Three Stage plays

by Colin Fantham

ISBN: 978-1-916596-99-3

The Final Chapter

of

A Strange Affair

A two act play

Written by **Colin Fantham**

<u>CHARACTERS</u>

Peter / George

Angela / Psychiatrist

Ken / Soldier 1

Brian / Soldier 2

Jacob / Minister

Belle / Nurse 1

Muriel / Nurse 2

Becky

Jonathon

George (Ten-year-old)

George (Late teenager)

Teacher

ACT ONE

Soulful music.

Peter's lounge. Decorated in smart late 1960s period style. Dimly lit.

> *Peter, a man in his sixties, wearing casual attire with cardigan, sits busily typing at his desk. He occasionally sips from his glass of whisky. He pulls the paper from the typewriter in frustration, rolls it into a ball, and throws it into the already overflowing bin. He replaces the discarded paper with a new sheet and stares at it, as though transfixed. He then rises in resignation, glass in hand, and stands by the window, looking out into the darkness beyond. Briefly, a vision in black and white of a ten-year-old Edwardian schoolboy is seen through the window. They exchange knowing glances. The vision slowly fades to darkness. Voices are heard eerily resonating throughout the room. Each sentence spoken is from a different voice originating somewhere from the writer's distant past.*

Voices   They forecast snow. There's something satisfying about seeing snow. Like a giant white comfort blanket. Makes even the grubbiest landscape seem appealing. It covers even the dirtiest of secrets. Don't you think? Makes life clearer. Less… *complicated*. You know where you are with snow.

Peter   They forecast snow. [*Enter Angela from staircase; she is in her early thirties, wearing smart colourful attire*] There's something satisfying about seeing snow. Like a giant white comfort blanket. Makes even the grubbiest landscape seem appealing. It covers even the dirtiest of secrets. [*Glances at Angela*] Don't you think? Makes life clearer. Less… *complicated*. You know where you are with snow.

Angela   You seem… preoccupied?

Peter   Thought I'd take a break. Waiting for inspiration. It's like waiting for a bus that's running late. [*Pause*] Maybe it's broken down?

Angela   It has been a while.

Peter   Too long.

Angela   All writers have dry spells.

Peter   This is more like a drought. I'm feeling my age. Withered. As though time was in short

supply.

Angela   Happens to the best of us.

Peter   Not you. You're as young as when I first met you. Still daisy fresh.

Angela   Only in your eyes.

Peter   Always in my eyes...

Angela   You always did have a way with words.

Peter   If I did, I wouldn't have a problem with the ending. It's like finding a needle in the

proverbial haystack.

Angela   All stories have endings. You just have to look for it. Probably just a phase.

Angela walks to coffee table and nonchalantly glances at magazine.

Peter   [*indignantly*] A phase? Teenage acne is a phase. This feels like an endless cycle of...

torment.

Angela   Isn't it all part of the creative process? It's what you do. It defines who you are.

Peter   I wish I could be so sure. I'm not as focussed as I used to be. The longer it goes on the

harder it is to finish it. I don't know if I have it in me anymore. Perhaps it's the end of the

road? No longer matters?

Angela   It matters to your Publisher. And your Agent. You know how much it means to *them*.

Peter   Parasites...

Angela   They may be. But you need them as much as they need you. It's a partnership. It's worked well in the past.

Peter   I feel like I'm losing my mind. The deadline has come and gone. Long ago. No doubt they'll be round for their pound of flesh.

Angela   There always has to be deadlines. Otherwise, nothing gets done.

Peter   They have no soul. It's no longer about the creative art. It's about the money. It's all they care about.

Angela   You shouldn't let it get to you. Take some time out. Away from here.

Peter   Time is no friend of mine. [*To himself*] Besides… easy for you to say.

Peter approaches radiogram, picks up sleeved LP and reads contents.

Angela   That hardly seems fair.

Peter   I'm sorry. You're probably right. You always were. Staring at blank sheets of paper all day is enough to make anyone mad.

Angela   Don't be so hard on yourself.

Peter   Why do I do it?

Angela   You have a talent, Peter. You just need to believe in yourself again.

Peter   I'm not sure I believe in anything anymore. Least of all myself. Nothing seems to make much sense these days.

Peter plays a slow instrumental jazz record on the radiogram.

Angela   You sound like a lost soul.

Peter takes large sip from his drink.

Peter   Maybe I am.

Angela looks around the room.

Angela   This place could do with a spring clean.

Peter   Why did you put up with me?

Angela   Because I loved you.

Peter   [*serious*] Likewise. Still do.

Angela looks to Peter with sadness in her eyes.

Angela   If only you had shown it more. Things might have turned out better.

Peter   I was always too preoccupied. I wasn't raised to show affection. Too… *English*, I suppose.

Angela   You've always struggled with your emotions. Kept everything in check. Not healthy.

Peter   It doesn't mean I didn't care.

Angela   Even so…

Peter   I often think back to when we first went out.

Angela   A lifetime ago.

Peter   That first date...

Angela   I remember it well. Not the most romantic of places, was it?

Peter   The Kings Head. I was terrified. Until I had a drink, of course. Funny how drink gives you courage.

Angela   Maybe it was me that drove you to drink?

Peter   [*shakes head*] I take full credit for that. I drove myself. My car always has at least a half

full tank of petrol. Maybe that makes me an optimist?

Angela   [*seriously*] Maybe that makes you an alcoholic?

Peter looks forlorn.

Peter   [*raises glass*] Guilty as charged.

Peter takes long drink.

Angela   Dad hated you. You were never good enough for his little girl. Mum said I should run a

mile. Too many years between us. Said it wouldn't work. That I should find a nice

Catholic boy. No money in writing.. No future...

Reflective pause.

Peter   She had a point.

Angela   And so we eloped. All those years ago. Without their blessing. I lived with them all my

life. Never even left the family home before then. And that was how I rewarded them.

They've never really forgiven me… Or you.

Peter   We caused quite a stir.

Angela   It *was* romantic. But insane. What were we thinking?

Peter   I was thinking… how lucky I am to be married to my young Irish beauty. You were

quite the catch for an old codger like me. We were happy. I don't think I've been

happier since.

Angela   We were happy. For a time... You spend far too many days looking back. You

should look forward more. To the future.

Peter looks vacantly at his drink.

Peter   I can't see past the bottom of this glass. Let alone the future.

Angela   You need to escape.

Peter   To where?

Angela   Anywhere but here. [*Looks around. Shivers slightly*] Too many memories. Too

many… ghosts.

Peter   Running away from here won't change what's happened. Besides… I've got to finish

it.

Angela   What if you *can't* finish it?

Peter   I've *got* to...

Angela shakes head in frustration.

Angela   You used to have such fire in you.

Peter   Fires have a tendency to go out... After a time.

Angela   Takes me back to when I was teaching. Trying to instil confidence into this one young

boy, an orphan, who I could see had potential. He was bullied remorselessly. The other

teachers thought he was a lost cause, but I could see he had talent. He wrote essays and

poetry, way beyond his years. I helped him as best I could. I was proud of him. I often

wonder what became of him. I miss that feeling of… value.

Thoughtful pause.

Peter   You were a beacon in a grey world.

Angela   And what of me now?

Peter looks to Angela with a tinge of sadness in his eyes.

Peter   It's been five years.

Angela   To the day.

Peter   I thought I could come to terms with it. Who was I kidding? I haven't been able to sleep.

I can't think straight. I *have* to find closure... If it's the last thing I do.

Peter rubs his forehead as if suffering from migraine.

Angela   You've lived with this inside you for so long…

Long pause.

Peter   Too long…

Angela   You're sick, Peter.

Peter   I know…

Angela   Maybe you should run a hot bath? Might relieve some of your discomfort.

Peter   No time. We have guests arriving soon.

Peter goes to drinks cabinet and tops up his drink. He takes out a small bottle from his

cardigan pocket and hurriedly takes a pill followed by a large sip of whisky.

Angela   Bad?

Peter looks to the heavens.

Peter   Bad enough.

Angela   You should see a doctor.

Peter shakes the bottle of pills.

Peter   Where do you think *these* came from?

Angela   Maybe you should think about retiring?

Peter   What would I do with myself?

Angela   Take up a hobby?

Peter   I was born to write. Too late to change now.

Angela   You need to unwind. Good for the soul.

Peter   You think I don't know? I have to live with myself every day. Alone with my thoughts. Memories that won't leave me. Voices... Not knowing anymore what's real and what's... insanity.

Angela   And me? You have to live with me every day. Maybe it's *because* of me?

Peter   I have to go on looking.

Angela   What is it you're looking for?

Peter   There's one piece of the jigsaw still missing. And it's not behind the settee. I've looked. I've looked everywhere.

               Long pause.

Angela   What do you hope to achieve by inviting them all over? It's not going to change anything.

Peter   I'll be the judge of that. [*Solemn*] Quite literally.

Angela   You really need to unwind. It's good for the soul.

Peter   I can't. Maybe later. When everything is clearer.

Angela   Maybe it won't be any clearer. What then?

Peter   I'll face that when I come to it.

Angela   You used to be so in control. Where's the man I used to know?

Peter   Things change. It's different now.

Angela   And me? Maybe I've changed?

Peter   You'll never change.

Angela   How can that be? You're not in the real world. We're born. We live. We age... We die.

It's the natural way of things.

Peter   Some things never die. Art. [*Gestures to radiogram*] Music. The written word.

Angela   Those are just things. They don't mean-

Peter   Love.

Peter and Angela look fondly at each other.

Angela   Writers. You're all quite mad.

Peter   Quite probably.

Angela   You can't go on like this. Where's it all going to end?

Peter   [*deflated*] I don't know. Not yet.

Angela   [*irritated*] And me. What about me?

Peter   Angela. [*Subdued*] Please...

Awkward silence.

Angela   You should never have read my diary. How *could* you?

Peter   Found it by accident. After all those years. It screamed out to be read. I couldn't help

myself. I didn't know you even *kept* a diary. You certainly had it well hidden.

Angela   It was private. Not for public consumption. What were you thinking?

Peter   I was your husband. Husbands aren't known for thinking. And we're not supposed to have secrets, either.

Angela   Everybody has secrets. Even you. You hide behind the characters in your books and think that nobody can see you? The *real* you? Nothing you do will change anything that's already happened. You can't control the past any more than you can control the future. You should have just ignored it.

Peter   Everything I thought was real was just… a lie. Not as clear cut as I imagined. How could I have been so blind? So much I didn't know. Until it was too late.

Angela   Some things should remain private. Forever.

Peter   I never meant to hurt you. I was always so busy trying to put words on paper that I forgot what was important in my life.

Angela   It's too late for that. What's done is done. It changes nothing.

Peter   I'm sorry. I was weak. Call it a moment of madness. Curiosity. It's a powerful force. Strong enough to kill a cat.

Awkward silence. Angela looks nonchalantly at pictures on walls and coffee table.

Angela   So many pictures...

Peter   I'd never dream of-

Angela   Why do we have so many pictures?

Peter   To remind me… I like to look at you. Us. It helps me to realise how lucky I was. I should have treasured all that I had. But I didn't. I let it all slip away. Took it for granted. And by then it was too late.

Angela   You really *do* live in the past.

Peter   It's safer there. It's where I belong. It's where *we* belong.

Angela   It's not a healthy way to live. You can only live for the future.

Peter   I've lived for the future. Highly overrated. Far easier living in the shadow of

days gone by. When life seemed to have a purpose. When there was hope. Instead of

despair. It seemed… safer. A complete myth of course. But it's a place where there are no

surprises. Nothing to bite you on the backside when you least expect it.

Angela   What about me? What about *my* future?

Peter   [*poignant*] We'll always have the past.

Angela looks around.

Angela   So many memories.

Peter   It's all I have left.

Angela   I hope you know what you're getting yourself into.

Peter   I'm not entirely sure I do.

Angela   Then why do it?

Peter   To find the missing piece.

Doorbell rings. Silhouettes of two guests seen through frosted glass of front door.

Angela walks up the stairs.

Angela   I hope you find it. For the sake of your sanity.

Exit Angela. Peter walks to front door.

Lights fade.

Soulful music.

An Edwardian school class, circa 1908. Door stage right. A large, framed photograph of King Edward VII is on left wall, adjacent to which is a door marked Headmaster. A wooden desk and chair within right of centre facing left. Centre left a larger desk with chair facing right. Large window on wall upstage centre. A blackboard on stand beside the larger desk with: "I will not hit other boys out of anger at this school" written in large letters in chalk.

> *Ten-year-old George sits at the smaller desk busily writing, while at the other desk sits a young female teacher, reading a book. The teacher puts book down and looks to George.*

Teacher   You are the limit, George. I can't think what came over you. They're so much bigger. It was never going to end well. It's all very well lashing out the way you did, but you have to consider the consequences. Mrs Peabody said her Johnny had a nose bleed for the rest of the day. [*George smiles proudly*] This is a serious matter. The school has strict rules governing behaviour of its pupils. When are you going to realise you can't take matters into your own hands? If you experience difficulties, you should bring it to the attention of a teacher. [*She stands and slowly approaches the boy*] Best keep your distance from those other boys. This is happening far too frequently. You seem to spend your entire life confined to these four walls. I'm beginning to feel more like a prison warden. My time is better spent teaching, rather than this. When will you ever learn?

George   Sorry, Miss.

Teacher   This is a good school, George. It has traditions. It has values. Oh, it may have its faults, just as we all do. But it will sustain you in the future. You're getting an education. A *good* education. You should learn to appreciate that. Embrace it. There are others who are not so fortunate. Don't waste this opportunity to make your life a better one.

George   Yes, Miss.

Teacher   [*looking over George's shoulder*] What is this?

The teacher picks up the paper from George's desk.

George   A story, Miss.

Teacher   That is not what you are supposed to be writing, as you well know.

George   I can't seem to help it. The words just seem to come into my head. I just write down
                  what I hear. Besides… it's beyond boredom writing the same line one hundred times.

Teacher   Then perhaps you are beginning to understand that actions have consequences.

George   Perhaps…

Teacher sighs, and puts paper back down.

Teacher   I have to confess, I often find merit to your stories, George, but during your
                  formative years there are rules that you have to abide by. Writing "I will not hit other
                  boys at this school out of anger" one hundred times, is one of them.

George   [*sheepish*]Yes, Miss.

Teacher   I know your… *circumstances.* [*To herself*] Only too well. But it's no reason to act the
                  way you do.

George   They call me names, Miss… Bad names.

Teacher   They are wrong to do that, and I have spoken to them on many occasions. Their
                  parents have also been informed of their cruel taunts.

George   And they push me. Like they had a *right* to. I was just defending myself.

Teacher   They are intolerable. You must learn, George, that because you are… *who* you are…
                  there will always be others in this world who regard themselves as somehow…

superior. It's no sin to be without a mother and a father. You have to understand that people can be like animals with the mentality of a herd. If they perceive weakness…

George   I hate them, Miss. And I hate this school.

Teacher   Everybody needs an education. You have to overcome your fears and learn as best you can. Your command of the English language is second to none in your class. You have a bright future. I know it seems dark now, but-

George   [*angrily*] I'll show *them*. Nobody will *ever* get the better of me. I'll fight them *all* if I have to.

Teacher   Fight them if you must, George. But not with your fists. Fight them with your words. You have a sharp mind. Use your skill and you'll have the upper hand. After all, isn't the pen mightier than the sword?

George   Yes, Miss.

Teacher   It's for you to learn how to rise above these false gods and use what talents I know you have, to make a better life for yourself in the future. [*The clock strikes five*] It's time for you to see the headmaster. [*George rises slowly from his chair, in trepidation, and walks towards the now-open door to the headmaster's office. The teacher walks gently beside George, and places a motherly hand on his shoulder as he walks through the door. The door closes. She walks back to George's desk and begins reading George's story, and smiles*] The Elephant that swallowed a mouse. How intriguing. [*Six strikes of the cane are heard. The teacher looks to the headmaster's office and shakes her head with emotion*] Intolerable.

Lights fade.

Peter's lounge. Jazz music coming from the radiogram.

Peter opens the door to his guests Ken and Muriel.

| Peter | Wasn't sure if you were coming. |

| Ken | You invited us. Not often I get to see my famous old brother. How are you? It's been a while. |

Peter smiles at Muriel.

| Peter | Muriel. |

Peter takes their coats and hangs them up in cloakroom. They enter the room.

| Muriel | Hello Peter. So nice to be out of the cold. I was just saying to Ken, we haven't seen you in ages, didn't I Ken? |

Peter closes front door.

| Ken | [*walks into middle of room*] See you're still into old fogey music. What's wrong with The Kinks? Or the Stones? Something with a bit of life to it. |

| Peter | That's for Bohemians. Like you. They won't last five minutes. |

| Ken | You need to get with it. They're about to put a man on the moon, and you're still living in the last century. You need to change with the times. |

| Peter | Let me get you a drink. Muriel? |

| Muriel | Gin and tonic, thanks. |

Peter goes to drinks cabinet. Glances at Ken.

| Peter | Beer? |

Ken nods assent. Looks to writing table.

| Ken | You're still working on it then? It's been a long time. |

| Peter | Doesn't seem to have legs. |

Ken   Maybe you should have chosen a different story?

Peter   Too far down the line.

Ken   You look tired. As though time has caught up with you.

Peter hands them their drinks.

Peter   I haven't been sleeping too well.

Ken   You need a break.

Peter   You're not the first to say that.

Ken   [*puzzled*] Hmm?

Muriel   [*now sat in armchair*] You're looking well. All things considered.

Ken   He needs to get out more. Tell him.

Muriel   I'm sure Peter's just fine aren't you, Peter.

Ken   Out in the real world.

Peter   I'm not sure I want to. I have a slender grip on reality these days.

Ken   Everybody needs to unwind. [*To Muriel*] Tell him.

Muriel   It might do you good to get away. A change of scenery?

Peter   I wouldn't know where to go. Besides, this is where I belong. Home is where the

heart is. Isn't that what they say?

Muriel   I suppose you're right. But all the same…

Peter   [*to Ken*] How's the rag trade?

Ken   It's called a newspaper.

Muriel   Ken's been moved to current affairs.

Peter   Oh? Whose current affair are you working on? Sophia Loren's, perhaps?

Ken   State of the unions.

Peter   Political journalism? You've got your work cut out. Everybody seems to be on strike

                 these days.

Ken   With good reason. Cheap labour coming in. New machinery. Workers being laid

                 off. Their only option is to strike to save their jobs.

Peter   Machines will never replace people.

Ken   Not if the trade unions have anything to do with it.

Muriel   The powers that be are trying to quash the unions. Even Barbara Castle. Makes me

                 ashamed to be a woman. And a labour supporter.

Peter   Surprised the red tops are being so socially adept. [*Replenishes his drink*] It's usually

                 about tits on page three.

Muriel   [*to herself in mild rebuke*] Really...

Ken   It's more than that. It's a paper for our times. A twentieth century reflection of

                 ourselves. That has to be a good thing.

Peter   Of course. I'm a bitter old man. Don't mind me. Can't seem to help myself.

                 I'm such a grouch. Must be in the genes.

Ken   You've got the old man's genes. He was always a grumpy old git. Bless him.

Muriel   Like chalk and cheese you two. Always were. Hard to believe you are brothers.

Ken   It's what we do. It's what we've always done. A family tradition. A regular

                 Cain and Abel.

Peter	That didn't end well, as I recall.

Ken   Mum was always telling me to be more like you. She could see you were the sensible one. Always abiding by the rules.

Peter   I think you broke every one of them.

Ken   There for the breaking.

Peter looks with contempt at Ken, who doesn't notice.

Muriel   It's been a long time, hasn't it? We should do this more often.

Peter   Absence makes the heart grow fonder. Isn't that what they say?

Muriel   True. But all work and no play makes Jack a dull boy.

Peter   [*raises glass*] Touché.

Ken   How long have you lived here, now? Ten years? You could have bought a mansion with all the money you've made.

Muriel   Ken. So insensitive.

Ken   Stop fussing. It's true. If I had your money…

Peter   Doesn't seem right to move. All my memories are here.

Muriel   Of course they are. Why would you want to move? Ken's just being silly.

Ken   I'd buy a country retreat. Somewhere to escape. Away from the big city. It would do you the world of good.

Muriel   Does sound attractive.

Ken   You need to get out more. Not good being cooped up in here all the time. If I had your money…

Long pause.

Peter   Sandwiches. [*Exits to kitchen*] I made sandwiches.

Muriel waits until Peter is out of earshot.

Muriel   Be nice.

Ken   I'm always nice.

Muriel   He's been through a lot. It's no wonder he's the way he is. Poor man.

Ken   We all have our trials and tribulations.

Muriel   But for a husband to go through *that*. Awful. Just awful.

Ken   It was years ago. Time he moved on. Time we *all* moved on. He's in a rut.

Not healthy.

Muriel   Poor man.

Peter returns with tray of sandwiches and lays them on coffee table.

Peter   Help yourselves.

Muriel   You shouldn't have gone to all that trouble, Peter.

Peter   The others should have been here by now. Hope the roads are okay.

Ken tucks into a sandwich.

Ken   Who else is coming? Didn't know this was a formal do.

Peter   I should have put some grit on the drive.

Muriel   It certainly is cold out there. Nice to see a real fire.

Ken   If I'd known I would have brought a bottle.

Muriel   Quite cosy really.

Doorbell rings. Silhouette of guest seen through frosted glass of front door

Peter   [*to Ken*] We've plenty of alcohol. [*Goes to front door*] Enough to sink a battleship.

Ken   [raises glass] Let the war begin.

Peter   [*opens door*] Hello.[*To the others*] You remember Brian?

Peter puts Brian's helmet and biker's jacket in cloakroom, and then closes door.

Brian   Bitter out. Lethal. Nearly went arse over tit.

Peter   Let me get you a drink.

Peter goes to drinks cabinet and pours wine into a large glass.

Ken   What bike do you ride these days?

Brian   Norton 650. Goes like the devil.

Ken   Still in the selling game, Brian?

Brian   Not at the moment. Let's just say I'm in between jobs.

Muriel   Oh dear. That's a shame.

Brian   Had a fall out with the manager. A real tosspot. Thought I had the wrong attitude. Didn't show enough respect to my elders and betters, he said. Silly old fart. Then he checked my qualifications. Not my fault I had a crap education. Sacked me on the spot. I could have been their top salesman given half the chance. [*Shrugs shoulders*] Their loss.

Peter   How many jobs have you had, now?

Brian   Five...? Feels like fifty.

Peter looks up.

Ken Too much of a free spirit.

Muriel [*chastising*] Ken.

Brian They'll never tie *me* down. Not if I can help it. Sod the lot of them.

Ken I don't blame you.

Peter How do you get by? [*Hands Brian glass of wine*] Where does the money come from?

Brian [*takes drink*] Oh, here and there. Buying and selling. [*Unsure*] Second-hand

goods? I get by.

Muriel Perhaps you should start your own business?

Ken Take out the middle man.

Peter It's knowing what to sell though. [*Looks knowingly at Brian*] Isn't that right, Brian?

Brian slightly flustered.

Brian I suppose so. Supply and demand.

Peter Give them what they need, eh?

Muriel You're still young. Haven't found your feet yet, I don't suppose. I'm sure you'll find a

job that suits you. Keep looking. You mustn't give up.

Ken Leave him alone. He's a free spirit. I'll drink to that. [*Goes to drinks cabinet and

helps himself to another drink*] Too many stuffed shirts in this world as it is.

Peter [*wry smile*] Company accepted.

Ken If I had my time again. You know what, Brian? I envy you.

Brian Me?

Ken   Footloose and fancy free. The world is your oyster. You get on your bike and let the wind take you where it wants. All I seem to be good for is paying the bills. I envy your freedom. [*Bitter*] Enjoy it while it lasts.

Doorbell. Silhouettes of two guests seen through frosted glass of front door. Peter goes to door and opens it.

Muriel   Lot to be said for a regular job. No offence Brian.

Brian   If they gave me a chance maybe I could hold down a job.

Ken   [*to Brian*] How do you like this music?

Brian   I'm more Jimi Hendrix really.

Peter lets in the next guests, who are a hippy couple in their early 30s, and closes front door.

Peter   Good to see you. Glad you could make it. Make yourselves at home.

Peter hangs up their coats and closes cloakroom door.

Jacob   [*rubs hands to get warm*] Intemperate weather for this time of year. You remember Belle?

Belle   [*slightly spaced out*] Hi all. Nice to be back in the warmth. [*Looks round*] Cosy.

Peter   I'll get your drinks. Jacob…?

Jacob   Beer thanks. Belle will have the same. [*Now by the fire*] Makes her feel empowering.

Ken   Still a feminist, then?

Belle   Afraid so. Does that threaten your masculine ideals?

Ken   No. Burnt your bra yet?

Belle   I don't wear one. Can't you tell?

Peter hands them bottled beers. Ken ogles Belle.

Muriel   [*indignantly*] Really. Young women today.

Brian   I thinks it's refreshing. Women's rights. Why not? Why should men have all the power? It's a new dawn. Stuff the lot of them.

Belle   Thanks Brian. [*Clinks her bottle against Brian's glass*] You always were a good friend.

Knowing look between the pair.

Peter   Help yourselves to sandwiches.

Belle   Starved. [*Examines sandwiches but realises they have meat in them*] Oh...

Ken   Still a veggie then?

Peter   Forgot. Sorry. Let me get you something else.

Belle   Don't bother on my account.

Peter exits towards kitchen.

Peter   Can't neglect my guests.

Peter now in kitchen.

Ken   Never understood anyone that doesn't eat meat. It's in our blood.

Belle   The thought of blood turns my stomach.

Ken   Why?

Belle   Goes against my principles. If it used to eat, walk, or shit, then I can't eat it.

Muriel   Why do women feel they have to use such profanity, these days? Honestly. Different in my day.

Ken   [*to Belle*] Animals were put on this earth to be eaten.

Belle   All creatures have a right to life. Just as you do.

Jacob   Don't mind Belle. She's political dynamite. If you stand too close, she may go off at any moment. You should have seen her at uni, debating the merits of left wing post-war feminism. The passion was *electric*.

Brian   I think freedom of expression is important.

Belle   Good for you, Brian.

Jacob   She was awesome. Everybody said so.

Muriel   I think everyone should know their place. Why does it have to be such a dog eat dog world? Good old-fashioned socialism. That's what this country needs. Everybody looking out for everybody else.

Belle   Give them an inch and they'll walk all over you. Women had to die before the establishment would even give us the vote. Don't think it couldn't happen again. One day we'll have equal rights.

Ken   That may be. But soon there won't be enough jobs to go round. Then what?

Belle   Then women will create more jobs. Given half a chance. Suppression is the evil of the twentieth century. But the shift of power is beginning to unfold. Just a matter of time.

Peter returns, and hands Belle a small plate of sandwiches.

Peter   Cheese and pickle. It was the only thing I could find that didn't eat walk or defecate.

Belle   Thanks Peter.

Belle tucks into sandwiches.

Muriel   Tell us about your new book, Peter. I've read your others. They're very good. What's it about?

Peter   [*reluctantly*] Difficult to say really. The usual things I suppose. Betrayal. Deception. Guilt. [*Uncomfortably*] It's unlucky to talk about an unfinished book. Let's just say it's a work in progress.

Peter goes to drinks cabinet and tops up his drink.

Muriel   Can't wait to read it. I must say I do enjoy a good murder. Seems to be a common thread through all your other work.

A look of recognition from Peter.

Jacob   The creative process is intriguing. Do you draw on personal experience?

Peter   [*more to himself*] More than you will ever know.

Muriel   It's almost as if you breathe life into the characters. They seem so real. You feel that you could reach out and touch them. They're so alive.

Brian   I remember years ago trying to read this book out loud at school. The Time Machine I think it was.

Jacob   H.G. Wells?

Brian   Yeah. Looked an interesting story. A cool picture on the cover. But the words just seemed jumbled up. It didn't make sense to me. It was like they had a mind of their own. Difficult to explain. The teacher thought I was an idiot. The other kids just laughed.

Jacob   You have to be in the zone for science fiction. Plays with your mind, man.

Brian   [*serious*] I don't think I've read a book since.

Brian looks blankly ahead in despondent thought.

Peter   Are you in the zone, Jacob?

[*Jacob looks puzzled*]

Belle   If you want a really good read, Brian, you should try Allen Ginsberg. He wrote a poem

called Howl. Fucking *brilliant*.

Muriel   Here we go again.

Ken   I've heard of him. Anti-this. Anti-that. Anti-everything. [*Disdainfully*] Yank. They think

they have all the answers that lot. Fat cigars and checked trousers. All the same.

Angela walks down the stairs, unseen.

Belle   It says everything you need to know about life. And love. I'll lend it to you if you like.

All except Peter are now perfectly still with heads slightly bowed. Even the music is

stuck as if continuously on the same note.

Peter   They haven't even mentioned you. It's as if you never existed. [*Angela enters room.*

Lights fade, except on Peter and Angela] As though you never had a life. [*Looks to*

Angela] Your very existence just… an inconvenience. Instead of a warm burst of

humanity that touched all of us here. Now just an irrelevance. Can't they see your

pictures? Are they blind? How can they be unaware of your absence? How can they be

so indifferent? Uncaring. It's so… insulting. Sad... What is *wrong* with these people?

They're so cold. [*Looks to others*] So inhuman.

Angela   They don't see things the way you do, Peter. [*Looks away*] Nobody ever does. They feel

awkward. Maybe embarrassed? I kept trying to tell you. It wasn't their fault. But you

wouldn't listen. [*Dismissively*] You never really listened. [*Emotional*] Even now when it's too late to change anything that's already happened, you're not really listening. [*Resigned*] Are you?

Peter   Of course it's their fault. [*Looks around at the others*] They're holding back because they know they have something to hide. It's like they're too afraid to face the truth. Of just how damaging their actions *really* were.

Angela   How can you be so sure?

Peter   Because each of them had a part to play. I know that now. It was your diary. [*Through the window we briefly see Angela's diary being opened with pages revealed*] They were your words. That's why I had to see each of them again. They can't live out their long lives without knowing what they did. To us. [*Pause*] To you. That wouldn't be right. They act as though nothing happened. I need to see this through. To its natural conclusion.

Angela   And what could you possibly hope to achieve by doing that?

Peter   Closure. I've lived with the betrayal, deception, and guilt for what seems an eternity.

Angela   Do what you have to do, but don't do it for me.

Peter   It has to be done. In my own way. To clear the air. Cleanse the soul. They can't pretend all is still normal. When it's clearly not. [*Angry*] I can't keep it bottled inside of me any more. I've lived in this… madness… for too long.

Angela   The only one at blame was me. Not them. [*Pause*] Not you. You should stop torturing yourself with this.

Peter   I believed that. For a long time. And then I think of your diary. Those words. Your words. They follow me everywhere. Every day. Every night. They changed everything. There's no escape. It's in the air. It's like a bad dream that never goes away.

Angela   It should never have happened. But it did, and that can never be changed. Not now. What's done is done.

Exit Angela

Peter   It's taken me a long time to confront this. Five years. Five long years. I was too blind and wrapped up in myself to see. But it's slowly becoming clearer.

Lights and sounds resumed as before. All continue their conversation.

Brian   [*to Belle*] Thanks but I don't think so. I can't guarantee I'll understand it. Sounds a bit highbrow to me.

Belle lights spliff and draws heavily on it.

Jacob   It's not to everyone's taste Brian. But it is still contemporary. You can feel his angst. It touches you in a way that no other writing can. You can feel the vibe. It's modern. Fresh. Authentic. He was a visionist. A radical poet.

Belle   He gives sight to the blind. [*Passes spliff to Jacob*] If only we could all see life for what it *really* is. It's not for the faint hearted. It's for the realists.

Brian   Might help me to see the real world?

Belle   Absolutely.

Ken   Cobblers. You make him sound like Jesus on the cross.

Muriel   Hear hear.

Ken   [*to Brian*] Don't be drawn into that claptrap. Their world is full of bullshitters. [*Disapproving glance from Belle*] It's true. It's like art. Picasso. People say he's a genius because he can paint women with wonky eyes and even wonkier tits. He's just a con artist who's been milking it for all it's worth. Toffy intellectuals giving too much credence to the creative arts. It's just pretentious twaddle if you ask me.

Belle   People need to open their eyes. There's a whole new scene out there.

Peter   Not everyone's cup of tea.

Muriel   I prefer traditional writers, like Dickens. I'm not keen on anything radical. People like to stir up a hornets nest. They think they are being so trendy. They're just being silly.

Peter slowly replenishes everyone's drinks.

Jacob   Not everybody's ready for change. But it's coming. Maybe it will take a revolution?

Peter   This is Stoke Newington. Not Petrograd.

Jacob   It's just a matter of time. Bob Dylan was right. Times are a changing. There's growing social and economic inequality. It's all around us. Maybe we should follow the French blueprint and overthrow the monarchy. Form a republic. And while we're at it overthrow the government. Excessive taxation is crippling this country. If they had their way they'd start taxing windows again.

Muriel   Not sure I'd want to live through a revolution. They never seem to end well do they? I'd like to keep my head firmly on my shoulders. I've become very attached to it.

Brian   Me too.

Belle   Don't worry, Brian. That's reserved for the bourgeoisie. The people who *think* they run this country. Not the workers.

Peter   [*dismissively*] He doesn't work. Not officially. Neither do you. You're still a student. [*Looks to Jacob*] Both of you. Funded by taxpayers. The workers. Me. When did you last do a day's work?

Jacob   It's everybody's right to an education, Peter. To broaden their mind. To explore cultures. Meet new people and challenge economic and political stagnation. To be a part of a progressive movement. To make a difference.

Peter How many degrees do you *need*? You have more letters after your name than there are in a Welsh *railway* station.

Muriel Do you mean like Llanfairpwllgwyngyllgogerychwyrndrobwllllantysiliogogogoch? [*Bewildered looks from all. Long pause*] My Mother was Welsh...

Jacob Times are a changing.

Belle The revolution's all around us. A sexual revolution. A peace revolution. A free speech revolution. [*Glances at Jacob*] We're part of a new movement. It's where things are really happening. A counterculture. We challenge boring conventions. By protesting in the streets. It liberates the soul to explore new possibilities. A new vision.

Ken A vision that's evolved from a cloud of psychedelic drugs? Not sure your mate Harold Wilson would approve.

Brian It's a different world now. We all have choices. If people want to take drugs, then so what? We should be able to make our own decisions.

Muriel Why do young people feel the need to take drugs? What's wrong with alcohol?

Brian Have you never felt the need, Muriel?

Muriel Good God no. Give me a gin and tonic any day. I can't imagine any drug being as comforting as a G and T. Some say gin makes them depressed. Well *I've* never been depressed. [*Contemplative*] Though, of course, I can get lonely. On occasion. That's a whole different thing, isn't it? I shouldn't really quibble. I'm very fortunate. Really. But some days can seem very long. Being a housewife. When you're all alone in the house. All day. Especially once the housework is done. A G and T is like a sedative. It has a calming effect. Like seeing an old friend again. I find it relaxes me. Makes the day seem more...bearable.

Peter refills his glass.

Peter   I'll settle for whisky. You know where you are with whisky.

Brian   All I know is, whisky makes you feel like death the next day.

                 Reflective pause.

Peter   Not if you drink enough of it.

                 Jacob rummages through Peter's record collection.

Jacob   Mind if I change the record?

Peter   [*to himself*] I wish you would. [*Gestures with hand*] Be my guest.

Jacob   Ah. Thought it was here. The Five Faces Of Manfred Mann. Fab. A classic if ever there
                 was.

                 Jacob plays the record.

Belle   Haven't heard that for a while. Brings back memories. '64 wasn't it?

Jacob   Great year.

                 Peter glares at Jacob.

Peter   A great *year*?

Jacob   [*motions to Belle*] Shall we?

Belle   Why not?

                 Jacob and Belle dance by the radiogram. Long pause.

Ken   [*lustily eyes up Belle*] She's quite the mover. [*Turns to Peter*] Thought you only had
                 stuffy old jazz records from the fifties?

Peter   Not all mine.

Ken ignores the pathos and continues to ogle Belle.

Ken   There's hope for you yet.

Brian   [*nods head to music*] Great music system, Peter.

Muriel   [*loudly tipsy*] I prefer The Beatles myself. Paul McCartney is *so* dishy. And such a

talented songwriter.

Peter collects Muriel's empty glass and tops it up.

Brian   I heard they were breaking up.

Muriel   No? That would be awful. Thought they would last forever.

Peter   Nothing lasts forever Muriel. People especially.

Peter watches Jacob and Belle dancing.

Brian   It's rumoured John Lennon's had enough. Wants to break out on his own.

Muriel   How sad. End of an era.

Brian   Some blame Yoko.

Muriel   Mad as a hatter that one. You can see it in the eyes. Shifty.

Brian   She's certainly eccentric.

Muriel   Eccentric? More egocentric I'd say. Has him wrapped round her little finger.

Brian   Do you think so? Can't see it myself.

Muriel   I think he's *mesmerised* by her. All that peace protest. In bed? I ask you. Is that

normal?

Brian   She is very…artistic.

| **Muriel** | I'll say. |

Pause.

| **Brian** | Fancy a shake? |

| **Muriel** | A dance? Oh okay. I'm not much of a dancer though. |

| **Brian** | Me neither. Two left feet. We're a perfect combination. |

Brian and Muriel put their drinks on coffee table and join Jacob and Belle dancing. Long pause.

| **Ken** | [*to Peter*] Silly old cow. Thinks she's seventeen. Making an exhibition of herself. |

| **Peter** | Why does it bother you? She's happy. You should be glad. |

| **Ken** | Making a fool of herself. Look at her. She's all *over* him. Embarrassing. She can't compete with Belle. Not many that could. Sexy bird, that one. |

| **Peter** | Still got an eye for other women, I see. |

Music fades. Light dims on all but Peter and Ken. Others with heads now bowed.

| **Ken** | Where's the harm? |

| **Peter** | Somebody else will always suffer. |

| **Ken** | Not if they don't find out. |

Peter takes long drink.

| **Peter** | I found out. |

A brief vision of Ken forcibly kissing Angela seen at window.

| **Ken** | [*unconvincingly*] Not sure I'm with you, old man. |

Ken takes long drink.

Peter   I know all about you...and Angela.

Long pause.

Ken   Oh...

[*Pause*]

Peter   I was away at a book signing when you decided to pay a visit.

Ken   I'd consigned that to the history book *years* ago. I'd forgotten all about it.

Peter   While the cat was away...

Ken   Didn't think you knew. [*Contrite*] It was a mistake. Call it human error.
Ancient history. [*Looks to Peter*] It meant nothing. To either of us. Forget about it.
[*Contemplative*] Long time ago. Water under the bridge.

Ken takes long drink.

Peter   Five years.

Ken   What do you want me to say? That I'm sorry it happened? I am. But it did. It makes no
difference. [*Solemn*] Not now she's gone. We were both in a bad place. Fucked up. We
didn't know what we were doing. And by then it was too late. You have to believe that.
Best left in the past.

Peter   She was my wife. You were my brother. Some might call that treachery.

Ken   Call it what you will. I'm not proud of what I did, and I'm sorry. But I can't turn back
the clock.

Peter   No. I don't suppose you can. And neither can I.

Ken   It meant nothing. A one off. I was drunk. She was as high as a kite. Maybe if

you'd paid her a little more attention it wouldn't have happened. Too wrapped up

in your own little world to notice how miserable she was.

Peter   You think I should be grateful to you?

Ken   No. Of course not. I often think about her. But you should take a long hard look at

yourself before blaming others.

Peter   I do. [*Drinks heavily*] Every day.

Lights and music resume. Ken walks to where Jacob and Belle are dancing and taps

Jacob's shoulder. Snow seen beginning to fall through the window.

Ken   May I?

Jacob backs off and Ken dances closely with Belle. Jacob joins Peter. Long pause.

Peter   Careful. He might steal her away from you.

Jacob   Belle? I doubt it.

Peter   I wouldn't be too sure. He's got previous.

Jacob   He's cheated on Muriel? Hard to believe.

Music fades. Light dims on all but Peter and Jacob. Others with heads now bowed.

Peter   He married for money. I think the novelty has worn off. You can tell he doesn't love

her anymore. He *despises* her.

Jacob   Pity. I rather like Muriel. Bit straight. But a kind soul. I can tell. She has a lot of love

inside.

Peter   Do you think you and Belle will ever get hitched?

Jacob   Marriage? It's a state institution. We don't believe in it. We don't need a piece of paper or a ring to prove our connection. It's an unwritten contract. Besides… love is free. It's like the air we breathe. We should all learn to love each other. The world would be a better place.

Peter   I'm not sure that life is ever that simple.

Jacob   You can't kill with love. Thousands are still dying in Vietnam. All because of hate. Hate never solved anything.

Peter sips from his whisky.

Peter   You were with Angela. At university.

Poignant pause.

Jacob   She was smart, Peter. Made it look easy. She took to politics and sociology like a duck to water. She really got how the nuances of hypocrisy tainted public life, you know? She was impressive. But I could sense she had a vulnerable side too.

Peter   In what way?

Jacob   Oh I don't know. She was like a butterfly. Caught in a net. I guess she just wanted to break free. But didn't know how. I don't think marriage suited her. Maybe she felt… stifled?

Peter   Stifled?

Jacob   She was a natural free spirit. [*Pensive*] I think marriage took that away. A part of her was lost. She said she never regained that sense of… independence… once she'd tied the knot. Her freedom of expression and movement was lost. Part of her succumbed to melancholy, I suppose.

Peter   Maybe if you hadn't subjected her to yours and Belle's…*unorthodox* lifestyle… she'd

still be here today?

A brief vision of Angela with Jacob and Belle smoking weed, is seen at window.

Jacob   I doubt that. We all see things differently. If anything it enabled her to express her

discomfort in a way she didn't feel able to do. I suppose we were a sort of outlet for her.

I always thought that Angela felt there was something missing in her life. Now that I

think of it, she seemed to have lost her spirit. You could see the magic drain from her

eyes. She was like a lost soul. [*Pause*] That was my take on it. Maybe I'm wrong?

Peter looks despondent.

Peter   Not the Angela I knew.

Jacob looks intently at Peter.

Jacob   When all is said and done, do we really know *anyone*, Peter?

Pause.

Peter   [*stares blankly ahead*] I'm beginning to wonder...

Lights and music resume. Jacob goes to drinks cabinet for another beer and watches the

dancers in silent contemplation. Long pause. Brian and Muriel return laughing by the

coffee table. Brian takes a sandwich. Muriel collapses, smiling, at the settee and closes

her drunken eyes.

Brian   Starved. She's knackered me out. She's got more energy than someone half her age.

Peter   That would be *you*.

Brian   She looks well on it. Marriage must agree with her.

Peter   I'm not so sure. What about you?

Brian   How do you mean?

Peter   Still young, free and single?

Brian   I'm happy enough. Still waiting for the right girl to come along. I like being single.

Enjoy the freedom it gives me. Means I can do what I want.

Music fades. Light dims on all but Peter and Brian. Others with heads now bowed.

Peter   And what do you *want* out of life, Brian?

Pause

Brian   I'm a simple soul, Peter. I enjoy life. To the max.

Peter   Some might say you ruin other people's lives.

Brian   How's that?

Peter leans in close.

Peter   You peddle dope.

Brian smiles uncomfortably. Long pause.

Brian   Means to an end. Supply and demand. Like you said. Needs must. If people didn't need

them, I wouldn't be selling. The world has changed since *you* were young. It's different

now. A new world. I've tried the usual way of making a living, but it's never worked

out. You don't know what it's like. Not being able to hold down a job before some

wanker decides I'm not good enough for them. I was left with no option. You have to

have money in this world to get what you want. It seemed the only avenue available to

me.

Peter   That doesn't make it right.

Brian   Sometimes you have to do what you have to do. To get by.

Peter   It's because of you that Angela had a habit. She came to you for her supply.

A brief vision of Angela taking drugs from Brian seen at window.

Brian   She was a free spirit. If it wasn't me it would have been somebody else. I've never

forced anyone to buy anything from me.

Peter   She would have been clean if it wasn't for you.

Brian   Let me ask you something.

Peter   Well?

Brian   You like whisky? [*Peter nods*] So much so that you can't get through the day

without it. It's like a *crutch* for you, isn't it? You get days when you try not to

take a drink but it's something that's with you all the time. It's inside you.

You can't fight it. You look in the mirror and it's there. When writing your books.

It's there. Even when you take a shit. It's part of you. I like you, Peter. But don't

lecture *me* about Angela. Take a long hard look at *yourself* before lecturing others.

[*Peter is strangely silent. Lights and music resume*] Now if you'll excuse me, I need the

little boy's room. I may even drop some acid. If that's alright with you?

Brian exits via staircase. Muriel rouses from her apparent slumber. She looks up to

Peter.

Muriel   I couldn't help but overhear.

Peter   How much?

Muriel   Most of it, I'm afraid. [*Sips from her drink*] I like Brian, but I certainly don't approve

of his lifestyle. If people want to ruin their lives with drugs that's their look out. He

should get himself a real job and stick with it.

Peter looks to staircase.

Peter   I'm not sure he'll *ever* be able to hold down a real job. I'm beginning to see that now…

Muriel   Maybe one day he'll grow up. See the error of his ways. Perhaps he's never had a role model? We all need somebody to look up to. Society seems to have turned its back on the Brians of this world. Washed its hands of them. You were young once. Didn't you ever do anything irresponsible?

Peter   I have a younger brother who has more than made up for my lack of juvenile indiscretions.

Muriel   He does have a certain boyish charm. Still has that fire in his belly. I suppose he's never really grown up. [*Smiles nervously*] Thinks he's Peter Pan.

Peter looks to Ken dancing with Belle.

Peter   Why do you stay with him?

Music fades. Light dims on all but Peter and Muriel. Others with heads now bowed.

Muriel   Because he's my husband.

Peter   Ah... The dutiful wife.

Muriel   Perhaps. I'm from a generation that doesn't just walk away when the going gets tough.

Peter   Some things are beyond the pale. Him and my wife, for instance.

Muriel looks to Peter in shock. Long pause.

Muriel   I didn't think you knew.

Peter   He betrayed you.

Muriel   And she betrayed *you*. It takes two, Peter.

Peter   How can you be so-

Muriel   Forgiving? I've learnt from experience. It's better that way.

Peter   And yet you couldn't find it in you to forgive Angela. She came to you. She begged

you…

A brief vision of Angela beseeching Muriel's forgiveness is seen at window.

Muriel   I told her I was going to tell you. But I couldn't bring myself. Perhaps I should have.

Maybe it would have resolved it. Cleared the air. I was scared. I suppose it took guts for

her to tell me. You could say I was a cold bitch. Maybe I should have forgiven her

there and then. But I couldn't. I'd been down this road before, you see. It's taken me a

long time. Ken is essentially a weak man. It's not the first time he's been… unfaithful.

It's in his nature. Ever since we were married he's been unfaithful to me. [*Looks to

Peter*] But he always came back. To me. They say love is blind. They say that for a

reason. It always hurts. There were days when I wanted to scream because it hurt so

much. They made a mistake. God knows we all make them.

Peter   You should have told me. Perhaps things would have been different. [*Pause*] She'd still

be here now.

Muriel   You can't put the blame on me, Peter. Maybe if you had paid more attention to her. In a

way a loving husband should... But you were always too busy, weren't you? Immersed

in your books. Immersed in your whisky. Drowning in your own world as always. Yes,

Ken might have his faults. He probably always will have. [*Pause*] But so do *you*.

*Lights and music resume. Muriel rises and gathers up some of the empty glasses from

the table and disappears into the kitchen. Ken and Belle stop dancing. Ken joins Jacob

and opens a fresh bottle of beer and is seen chatting with him. Belle joins Peter by

coffee table and devours the last of her sandwiches. The music continues in

background.*

Belle   Where's Brian?

Peter   Boys room. [*Pause*] Why?

Belle   [*anxiously*] He's got something for me.

Long pause.

Peter   Why do you do it, Belle?

Music fades. Light dims on all but Peter and Belle. Others with heads now bowed.

Belle   [*coyly*] Because it makes me feel free. Free from the real world. It makes me feel like I'm in a different place. A place that isn't fucked up. For a while at least. It's a place where colours are so… vivid. You know? They blow your mind. Blurs reality. Makes you forget all the *shit* that's happening out there.

Peter   Is the real world really that bad?

Belle   Just look around you. There's an explosion waiting to happen. People should have rights. Exploitation is everywhere. People afraid of losing their jobs if they speak out. Women still being subjugated simply because of their sex. But things will change. It's just a matter of time.

Peter   You have a very cynical outlook. I'm no longer sure that time changes anything.

Belle   [*light-heartedly*] Now who's being cynical?

Peter   [*subdued*] You knew Angela. You were close at one time.

Belle   [*sadly*] She was a good friend. I still miss her.

Peter   Such a good friend that you introduced her to Brian?

A brief vision of Angela and Belle accepting drugs from Brian is seen at window.

Belle   It's a free world Peter. Angela was her own woman. She had her own mind.

Peter   The drugs destroyed her mind. She became a different person. Not the woman she was.

Belle   And you blame *me*?

Peter   Maybe if she hadn't met *you* things might have been different.

Belle   Life doesn't work that way. You can't control it.

Peter   Life should have a sense of order. Otherwise it's just anarchy.

Belle   Life *needs* anarchy. Sometimes. You have to shake it by the throat in order to get

change. Otherwise it's just stagnant. Going nowhere.

Peter   Angela had a *life* before she met you.

Belle   Angela had a richer life for having met me. Oh, I only knew her for a short time but I

know that she was happy. For a while. Probably lived a life more fulfilling in the short

time I knew her than when she was married to you. She felt trapped, Peter. With

nowhere else to go.

Peter   [*earnest*] I had more love for her than you could ever know.

Belle   That may be. But you kept that to yourself. Hidden inside. Like you always did.

Like you always *do*. She was starved of the attention she needed from you. The spirit

that was inside her just drained away. Until there was nothing left. [*Sad pause*] Until it

was too late.

Belle exits via the stairs in search of Brian. Long pause. The light remains on Peter.

Jacob and Ken are still. Enter Angela. The snow outside is seen to be falling heavily.

Peter   I've been such a fool. I thought I would have closure. I assumed it was all their fault.

That if I could somehow pin the blame on each of them... But I was wrong. It wasn't all

of them. [*Pause. Looks to Angela*] It was only one. And now I have to live with that.

Inside of me. Like a darkness.

Angela   It doesn't have to be like that. Erase it all from your mind. You can still move on with your life. Look forward. Not back. You just have to free yourself from all of this…madness. You have to find a way to end this, Peter. One way or the other. Otherwise you will never find peace.

Peter   [*looks blankly ahead*] There *is* only one way. I can see that now. Maybe then I can escape the demons living inside my head. Words. Words that resonate. *Your* words. Reverberating. They're here now. Can't you see them?

Extracts from the diary are seen repeatedly through the window: Made friends with Jacob at Uni. Belle introduced me to Brian. Ken seems attracted to me. Peter shows no affection anymore. Need new supply from Brian. Lost my job today. He RAPED me!!! Losing my mind. Why did I let Ken in??? Peter so cold to me now. Muriel has threatened to tell Peter. The drugs have taken my soul. Morning sickness! Please God no!!! My life isn't worth living anymore. I just want to die. I just want to die!!!

Angela   Yes, I see them.

Peter   Every day is the same. Swirling like leaves in the wind. There's no escape. I don't think they'll ever leave me alone. It's a *madness*. Like a poison. Eating away at my soul. Always inside of me. [*Pause*] Until I can end it. Once and for all.

The words fade.

Angela   I was in a dark place. Everything somehow spiralled out of control. Everything that happened was my own fault. It's time to let go.

Peter   I can't…

Angela   Life is for the living. Not the dead.

Exit Angela.

Peter   If only that was true…

Lights and music resumes.

Jacob   [*to Peter as he walks to front door*] The weather's getting worse. It's snowing buckets. I'll have to check on the car. The old banger's nearly on its' last legs.

Peter   I know the feeling…

Exit Jacob. Ken and Peter are now alone.

Ken   I'd better do the same.

Ken begins to walk to door.

Peter   Wait.

Ken stops and looks to Peter.

Ken   Well?

Long uncomfortable pause.

Peter   Join me for one last drink? Old time's sake.

Ken   What's the point? I think we've said enough.

Ken walks towards the door.

Peter   Wait. You don't have the full story.

Ken again stops in his tracks and looks to Peter.

Ken   Well?

Peter   She was pregnant, Ken.

               Peter goes to drinks cabinet and pours Ken a large glass of whisky.

Ken   What are you saying? That it was mine? Are you *insane*?

Peter   It's quite likely that I am. But the truth of the matter is that she was carrying your

               child. [*Long pause*] Think you may need a drink.

               Peter raises Ken's glass

Lights fade.

Soulful music.

School class, as before, now circa 1916. A framed photograph of King George V is on left wall.

               George's teacher is seen packing away her personal belongings from her desk

               into a bag. Her eyes are wet with tears. Enter George, now a late teenager, from right

               door.

Teacher   [*notices George*] It's customary to knock before entering, George.

George   [*slightly breathless*] You're leaving, Miss?

Teacher   You should be on your way home. Your people will be worried about you.

George   You've been crying?

Teacher   [*dries her eyes quickly with a handkerchief*] It's nothing. I think I may have a cold.

George   Where will you go?

Teacher   I've volunteered to join the British Red Cross. There's a convalescent home not far

               from here for the war wounded to recuperate. I'll be working there.

George   But why? You're a teacher. A good teacher. You're needed here.

Teacher   The way this wretched war is going they will need all the help they can get. I have some training in first aid, which should be of value. [*Pause*] I really didn't believe there would even be a war. Such an evil waste of people's lives. [*Looks about her*] I will miss this place. [*Looks to George*] And all my boys. The school may have its faults and god knows there are many I don't agree with [*looks briefly towards the headmaster's office*] but I have found some satisfaction to be gained from teaching. I will miss reading your stories George. So...*expressive.*

George   I can't imagine you not being here. It doesn't seem... right.

Teacher   You're a young man now George. You have your whole life ahead of you. This is your last term. You'll soon forget me. And all the other teachers.

George   [*earnestly*] I could never forget you. You're the only one that's ever given a damn about me. [*Angrily*] The others can all go to *hell.*

Teacher   [*mildly rebuking*] Not the language befitting a young gentleman.

George   When will you return?

Teacher   [*pensive*] That rather depends...

George   I can't bear the thought of you... leaving.

Teacher   You'll soon be finding your own way in the world, George. Finding suitable employment. Maybe settling down? It's all part of the growing process, after all. Perhaps this war will be over soon. Then sanity can resume. And we can all live normal lives again.

George   [*bewildered*] Normal?

Teacher   You've come a long way, George. You've risen above your... *anxieties*. I've always

admired your spirit. Your tenacity. [*Warmly*] Even though it has been misplaced, on

occasion.

George   It's not *fair*. You're the only good thing that's ever happened to me. Everything else...

Teacher   I know things seem somewhat dark. That's because of this war. Nothing seems to

make much sense these days. Everything has been turned upside down. Why people feel

the need to kill each other has always mystified me. It's so... barbaric. Whatever

happened to loving thy neighbour?

George   You don't have to go.

Teacher   [*more to herself*] But I do. You don't understand.

George   [*petulant*] It's not *fair*...

With her bag now packed, the teacher stands before George.

Teacher   [*vacantly*] I suppose this is goodbye.

Air raid warning whistles are heard in the distance.

George   Don't leave. [*Pause*] Please... Stay.

Teacher   [*panicked*] What? George... the whistles. That means the zeppelins must be overhead.

We need to take shelter.

George   This school *needs* you. They'll never find anyone to replace you at such short

notice.

Teacher   [*sadly*] They already have. [*Pause*] This school will cope perfectly well without me. In

fact the headmaster-

The sound of zeppelin engines are heard overhead.

George   I need you.

Teacher   What? But that's- George… the whistles.

George   [*simply*] I love you.

Teacher   [*confused*] Don't be foolish George. You're just- You're just-

The sound of a bomb whistling towards them overhead. The teacher reaches out protectively to George, who holds the teacher. George kisses the teacher who tries to break free but is unable. The bomb is heard going off close by. A distant flash from the explosion seen at the window as the classroom lights go out. The teacher breaks free from George and they stand staring blankly at each other, silhouetted against the burning light outside.

Lights fade.

End of Act One.

ACT TWO

Soulful music.

A dark bleak windswept graveside, circa 1917.

We see the Minister far left presiding over an open grave. Strewn before the grave to the right are the congregation consisting of: Red Cross nurse 1; Red Cross nurse 2; Soldier 1; Soldier 2. Soldier 1 has a bandaged head and leans on a crutch. Soldier 2 has an arm in a sling and holds a walking stick by his side. Their heads are bowed. The dishevelled figure of George enters far left on his own, looking on with a bouquet of flowers in his hand.

Minister   Into your hands O merciful Saviour, We commend your servant Angela Jenkins, Acknowledge, we pray, a sheep of your own fold, A lamb of your own flock, A sinner of your own redeeming. Enfold her in the arms of your mercy, In the blessed rest of everlasting peace, And in the glorious company of the saints in light.

All   Amen.

Minister   Would any here today like to commit a few words before we lay Angela to rest?

Nurse 1   Angela was like a sister to me. Although I only knew her for a short time I could see that she was principled, brave, and always did what was right. She didn't deserve to die the way she did.

Nurse 2   Hear hear.

Soldier 1   It's in our blood to fight wars. And to win them. But now I see the futility of it all, father, and it makes me sick to the stomach with shame. She tended to my needs, and for that I give thanks. I will always remember her.

Soldier 2   She was an angel that helped a simple soul like me in my hour of need. She gave me

comfort and hope in this miserable dark world when I needed it the most. I will never

forget her kindness.

Minister   [*to George*] Young man. Join us. Perhaps you have a few words?

George   [*nervous*] I… I'm not comfortable making speeches, sir.

Nurse 2   Don't be afraid. What's your name lad?

George   George.

Soldier 1   You heard the Minister. Speak up. Say a few words.

George   [*shakes head*] I wouldn't know what to say...

Nurse 2   Just say whatever comes to mind, George. Take your time.

George   [*looks to others*] She was my teacher. A long time ago.

Nurse 1   [*accusingly*] You look familiar to me. Do I know you?

Worried look from George.

George   Maybe I should leave-

George turns as if to leave.

Nurse 2   Stay. Say your piece.

George   Well… She was a kind person. In a time and place where I hadn't known

much kindness. She taught me to rise above the failings of others. Be true to myself.

Nurse 2   Well said.

Nurse 1   She was too kind.

Minister   I'm not sure this is the time-

Nurse 1   Too trusting.

Nurse 2   The Minister's right. This isn't-

Nurse 1   [*emotional*] Found with a rope round her neck? She didn't deserve that. Nobody

deserves that. After all she did for King and country. Her life cut short the way it was.

What sort of animal treats another like that?

Soldier 1   If I could get my hands on him…

Soldier 2   They should line him up and shoot him.

Soldier 1   I'd kill him myself. [*Looks to others*] With my bare hands. Bastard.

George clutches the sides of his head as if trying to block out sound.

Nurse 2   He must be sick. Who could do such a thing?

Soldier 1   Somebody out there knows him. You can be sure of it.

Minister   Do we really know anyone, my son? The Lord will judge those who commit evil

deeds on that fateful day.

Nurse 1   The whole world is sick, father. So many evil deeds are being done. All in the name of

a justifiable war. How can the Lord judge so many people when the whole *world's*

gone mad?

Nurse 2   Death and destruction everywhere. It's not right, living like this. In a living hell.

Where is the peace we were promised? When will it all end?

Soldier 2   When we've killed every last one of them.

Soldier 1   And what then, lad?

Soldier 2   Then we win, and it will be done. If we don't kill them, they'll kill us. It's as simple

as that.

Soldier 1   You're a bloody fool. Nobody wins. This isn't a game.

Nurse 2   What sort of a world will our children live in? There'll be nothing *left* for them.

Minister   We are all god's children.

Soldier 2   What sort of a god lets this happen?

Minister   He works in mysterious ways.

Nurse 1   I'm not sure he's *my* god.

Minister   We must have faith.

> *Soldier 2 looks at George, suspiciously.*

Soldier 2   Why aren't you in uniform?

Nurse 1   You look like you've been sleeping in a ditch.

> *George looks defensively at others.*

Nurse 2   He's just a lad. Leave him be. A good lad too. He came to pay respects.

George   [*distant*] I…I tried…joining up… but they said… they said…

Nurse 2   Too young, I expect.

George   Yes…I expect that was it, really.

Nurse 1   I've seen you from somewhere.

George   I… I think you're mistaken.

Soldier 1   Leave him alone. He's a good lad.

Nurse 2   Wish there were more like you, George. This world would be a kinder place.

Soldier 2   In a time like now do you think the hun will be beaten by kindness? They only recognise hate, slaughter, and blood.

Minister   Whoever says he is in the light and hates his brother is still in darkness.

Soldier 2   I hate them as much as they hate me, father. And that's the way of it.

Minister   The Lord our god is merciful and forgiving, even though we have rebelled against him.

Nurse 2   Amen to that.

Soldier 1   Merciful? [*Louder*] Merciful? I've lost many a friend from this conflict. We were brothers in arms. They were shown no mercy but brutally dispatched from this world by hatred. Where was god when *they* needed him?

Soldier 2   [*gestures to grave*] Where was god when *she* needed him?

Nurse 1   After all she did. It beggars belief.

Nurse 2   She never talked about her relations. Did she have family, father?

Minister   Her parents died when she was very young. She was brought up as an orphan in the local Parish orphanage.

George looks distraught.

George   She was an orphan...

Nurse 2   What of it, George?

George looks to others as if seeking solace.

George   I didn't know... She kept that to herself.

Minister   She was probably too proud to admit that she was without parents. In the end we are all of His flock.

George   That accounts for it.

Soldier 1   Accounts for what?

Nurse 1   [*to George*] I've seen you. Coming out of Angela's residence.

George   No... I think you're mistaken...

Nurse 2   Perhaps you may know more as to why she died, George?

Soldier 2   If you know anything, now is the time.

George   [*shakes head*] We were... friends. I don't know why she died. [*Looks to others*] Really I
don't.

Soldier 1   I thought she was your teacher.

George backs away slightly from others.

George   I also considered her my friend.

Nurse 1   Why are you even here? You're just a kid. Angela was a grown woman.

Nurse 2   If you know anything, George...

George   I came because it seemed the right thing to do. [*Loudly*] I don't know why she
died. [*Looks to others*] I swear.

Soldier 2   He doesn't even wear the King's uniform. Why should we believe anything *he* says?

Minister   This is not the time for groundless recriminations. The boy came to pay his respects to
the dearly departed.

Nurse 1   This is the perfect time, father. He has some explaining to do.

Nurse 2   We are not here to judge George for attending his friend's passing. I'm sorry, George.

Nurse 1   Sorry? Angela is six feet under and you're *sorry*?

George   I should go.

Soldier 1   You don't have to leave, lad.

George   Voices...

George drops the flowers and runs away. Others shout almost in unison.

Minister   Stay, my son. Don't leave in this way. We are all god's children.

Nurse 2   George. George. Be sensible lad.

Nurse 1   You can run but you can't hide. Not for long.

Soldier 1   Stay lad. Stay. You don't need to be afraid.

Soldier 2   Somebody should stop him. SOMEBODY...

Lights fade.

Soulful music.

Peter's lounge.

Peter is seen holding Ken's drink aloft while Ken stares at him in disbelief.

Ken   Pregnant? What are you talking about? That's a lie.

Peter shakes his head.

Peter   It's the truth.

Ken   [*dismissively shakes head*] It must have been yours. You're wrong. She was never in the club. You're a bloody liar. Letting that writer's imagination of yours run away with you.

Peter   I found her diary. It was there in black and white. Besides...I can't have kids. Bodily impairment. [*To himself*] One of many.

Ken   [*despairingly*] Pregnant?

Peter approaches Ken, and hands him his drink.

Peter   You must have known it was a possibility?

Ken   I was so drunk. I didn't even consider…

Peter   The consequences? All actions have consequences. Separates us from the beasts. At

least it should.

Ken   How long have you known?

Peter goes to the drinks cabinet to top up his glass.

Peter   Feels like a lifetime.

Ken   And it's been eating away at you. For all this time.

Peter   Time has not been a healer.

Ken   What do you want me to say?

Peter   Nothing you can say or do will bring her back.

Ken   It was so long ago, Peter.

Peter   Not for me. Time seems to have stood still.

Ken in deep thought.

Ken   Pregnant… The irony...

Peter   Irony?

Ken   [*incidentally*] Muriel wanted kids. But it never happened. And now it's too late.

Ken takes long drink.

Peter   [*wryly*] It was very careless of you.

Ken   It just… happened. I told you. If I could turn back the clock-

Peter   But you can't. Believe me, I've tried.

Ken   Why torture yourself with the past? What's done is done. [*Loud*] She walked out on *you*

             five YEARS ago… and never came back. [*Pleading*] What's that got to do with *me*?

Peter stands by the drinks cabinet.

Peter   [*distant*] Everything...

Ken   This is insane. You need to let go and just get on with your life. On with your work.

             Nothing we say or do will ever bring her back.

Peter   I find it hard to just let go. You don't understand. It feels like she's still here. Every day.

             Like a ghost. Can you imagine what that's like, Ken? I wake up in the morning and she's

             there. I talk to her, and she talks back. It's as though she's still here. [*Long pause*] Maybe

             I'm mad? I can't distinguish between fact and fiction. Nothing makes sense anymore.

Ken   You're ill, Peter. You need help. [*Looks around the room*] You should get away from

             this place. It's unhealthy.

Peter shakes head in resignation.

Peter   It's too late for me. Too late...

Ken   Why?

Peter   Last roll of the dice.

Ken   What do you mean?

Peter   Intracranial neoplasm.

Ken   What the hell is that?

Peter   I have a lump on my brain.

Ken   Can't they just remove it?

Peter   Not that simple. Abnormal cells. Nothing they can do.

Ken   I had no idea. I'm so sorry. [*Feels dizzy*] I'm sorry for everything. You have to believe me.

Pause.

Peter   [*solemn*] I'm sorry too...

Ken suddenly feels weak.

Ken   I feel so... I need to sit down.

Ken slumps into the armchair.

Peter   It's the whisky. It's not a drink that takes kindly to strangers. [*Pause*] Takes years of practice to become its friend. Believe me. [*Sombre*] Drink up.

Ken empties his glass, and Peter refills it from bottle.

Ken   I'm not sure this is a good idea.

Peter returns to drinks cabinet and replaces bottle. He refills his own glass from another bottle.

Peter   Do you remember when we were kids?

Ken   Of course.

Peter   You were always getting into trouble.

Ken   Some things never change.

Peter   You never played by the rules.

Ken   There to be broken.

Peter   That's you in a nutshell. Your whole life. Doing whatever Ken wanted. Not giving a shit

about anybody else.

Ken   You were always Mother's pride and joy. I feel like I've lived in your shadow my whole

life. Maybe it's the age difference. I was never good enough for her and the Old Man.

Too busy enjoying myself to care about them. With Dad dying, I suppose you tried to

fill his shoes. That must have been hard for you.

Peter   It was. [*Lost in thought*] They were very *big* shoes.

Peter goes to the pile of records by the radiogram and picks up an LP record and

nonchalantly reads the sleeve cover. Ken takes large drink from his glass.

Ken   You said you found her diary?

Peter   Hmm?

Ken   Why didn't you give it to the police?

Peter   Why would I do *that*?

Ken   Evidence. [*Pause*] Surely?

Peter   Nothing was going to bring her back.

Ken   Maybe it would have at least given a clue as to where she went.

Peter   [*shakes head*] Too late in the day.

Ken   Maybe they could have found her by now? [*Pause*] Unless-

Peter   Unless?

Long pause.

Ken   Unless you killed her.

Pause.

Peter   I didn't kill her. [*Looks to Ken*] You did.

Ken   Me? That's insane.

Ken begins to feel very unwell.

Peter   If it wasn't for you, she'd still be alive.

Ken   What? You don't even know that she's dead. She walked out on you. [*Dismissively*] You don't know what you're saying.

Peter   She was already at death's door. A shadow of herself. Body riddled with drugs. Day after day. Depression. I no longer recognised her. [*A vision of Angela in the throes of deep drug addiction is briefly seen at the window*] I couldn't bear to see her like that. Not the woman I married. The woman I loved. You see, she wanted to die. It was in her diary. It seemed a humane thing to do. Smothering her while she slept. Strange... she finally looked at peace with the world.

Ken   You killed her.

Peter   You left me no choice.

Ken   You could have helped her.

Pause.

Peter   I did.

Ken   [*emotional*] She didn't have to DIE.

Peter   The woman I loved had already died. Inside. Thanks to you. She couldn't live with the consequences. All actions have consequences. You *raped* her.

Ken   [*slurring*] Where is she? What did you *do* with her?

Peter   Disposed of. Buried. Far away. Got rid of all the evidence. Even the diary. Better if her parents thought she had gone away. *Far* away. I knew her handwriting well enough to write a convincing note. And all because of my little brother.

Ken   I think I'm going to be sick. [*Stands*] Where are the others…? I need some air.

Peter   I poisoned your drink. Just as you poisoned Angela with your semen.

Ken   What?

Ken goes to front door but is unable to open it because of his frailty.

Peter   An eye for an eye. Isn't that the saying?

Ken   You're mad.

Peter   All writers are mad.

Ken collapses lifeless by the front door.

Lights fade.

Soulful music.

A dimly lit psychiatrist's office. Circa 1917.

The psychiatrist sits in an easy chair on left facing George, centre right, who sits upright on a black armless chair. George is wearing the uniform of a prison inmate: a pale buttonless jacket and matching trousers, pale laceless shoes and no socks; his hands and ankles are chained. The office is bleak. A lightbulb hangs from a long wire that shines down upon George, and is swinging slightly. The psychiatrist holds a clipboard and makes notes.

Psychiatrist   You seem… preoccupied. Tell me about the voices, George?

George looks to the psychiatrist as though he has just woken from a sleep.

George   They tell me things. Sometimes. I try hard not to listen. But even if you ignore them, it doesn't make them go away.

Psychiatrist Can you hear them now?

George nods.

George   Whispers. It's not always clear what they're saying. I… I try to block them out. As best I can. Easier said than done.

Psychiatrist You say they tell you things. What sort of things do they tell you?

George   I wouldn't like to say. I've learned to live with them. As I said I try to block them out. But sometimes they're very… persistent. [*Puzzled look*] I feel like I know them. Their voices seem *familiar* to me. From somewhere. Most of the time I ignore them but then they carry on as if I wasn't there. [*Smiles slightly*] You must think that very strange.

Psychiatrist I find nothing you say strange, George. I'm here to listen. To help you.

George   They tell me to do things. Sometimes they seem angry with me. At least… until…

Psychiatrist Yes?

Pause

George   [*sad*] Nothing.

Psychiatrist I can't help you if you don't open up, George.

George   Can I leave now?

Psychiatrist Tell me about your childhood memories.

George   Not much to tell.

Psychiatrist Was it a happy time of your life?

George   Happy? [*Long pause*] I was always running away. Never really settled anywhere.

Psychiatrist Who were you running from?

George   [*distant*] Everybody.

Psychiatrist Why?

George   Because everybody is fake.

Psychiatrist In what way?

George   They pretend to be your friend and then you realise they're just… pretending. They've always let us down. Seems to be a constant theme in my life. Just when you think you know someone they become… *different*.

Psychiatrist [*busily writing*] Interesting...

George   Hmm?

Psychiatrist You said *us*.

George   [*blankly*] Did I?

        Long pause.

Psychiatrist Why do you think people always let you down?

George   Because they don't care. Not really. There are always… other agendas.

Psychiatrist How do you mean?

George   They want something in return. Usually something bad.

Psychiatrist And you feel threatened by these people?

        George glares at psychiatrist.

George　　Of course. Who wouldn't?

Psychiatrist　When did you first start to hear the voices, George? Where did they come from?

George shakes head vigorously.

George　　I can't. Too awful. Please...

Psychiatrist　It might help...

George　　Some people are beyond help. Don't you think? Why are you wasting your time on me for? I'm a lost cause.

Psychiatrist　This isn't about me. It's about you. Nobody is a lost cause. [*George seems preoccupied*] Are the voices talking to you now?

George　　Yes.

Psychiatrist　What are they saying?

George　　[*nervously*] They're telling me to leave.

Psychiatrist　You're safe here George. You don't have to go anywhere.

George　　That's easy for you to say. You don't have to live with them.

Psychiatrist　They're not real, George.

George　　[*serious*] They're real to *me*.

Long pause.

Psychiatrist　I'm told by the wardens that you write?

George　　Stories. Lots of them.

Psychiatrist　Tell me about that.

George   My teacher encouraged me. It takes me to a different place.

Psychiatrist That's good, George. [*Pause*] Tell me about your teacher.

George   She's… dead. I can't tell you any more about her. Please don't ask me. I can't...

Psychiatrist She must have been very special to you.

George   [*sad*] She was.

Psychiatrist You know why you're here?

George   They told me I killed her.

Psychiatrist And did you?

George   I suppose I must have. They seemed very sure.

Psychiatrist What do you write about?

George gently rocks back and forth.

George   Just stories.

Psychiatrist I'd like to read them some day.

George   I really don't think-

Psychiatrist We're making progress, George. Tell me about your stories. What are they about?

George   The usual things. Betrayal. Deception. [*Pause*] Guilt.

Psychiatrist Interesting. [*Makes notes*] And does that help with your… anxieties?

George   Yes. Until I finish what I'm writing. Then I'm back to square one again.

Psychiatrist And while you're writing, you no longer hear the voices?

George   It's the voices that tell me what to write.

Psychiatrist   I don't understand.

George   I rely on them to write my stories. I hear what they say, and I simply write it down.

Psychiatrist   Have you tried writing your stories on your own? Without the voices?

George   I *told* you. Without them I *have* no stories. I *rely* on them.

Psychiatrist   Intriguing. [*Pause*] George, I want to arrange for you to undergo a new treatment. It's

                   for people with your… *condition.*

George   Treatment?

Psychiatrist   Electroshock therapy.

George   You want to fill me with electricity?

Psychiatrist   It *is* pervasive, but it may help.

                   George hears voices and stands up as if to leave.

George   They're telling me to leave.

Psychiatrist   [*rises*] You don't have to do as they say. The voices are not real.

George   They *are* real. They're here now. [*Looks to psychiatrist*] They're here NOW.

                   George covers his ears. We hear whispered incoherent voices getting louder.

Psychiatrist   Listen to me. They're *not* real. They're just a figment of your imagination. A delusion.

George   There's no escape from them. You don't *understand*. I'll never be free. Not now.

Psychiatrist   We can help you.

George   I must leave… I MUST.

Psychiatrist   I'm afraid that won't be possible George. [*Long pause*] Not for a long time.

George looks to psychiatrist in fear. Voices fade.

Lights fade

Soulful music.

Peter's lounge.

> *After an interminable wait, the doorbell interrupts George's silent contemplation as he sits in the armchair.*

George   [*slurring*] What…? What do you want? Leave me alone. Not now. [*Doorbell rings. The snow has now stopped falling, and faint daylight is seen emerging from the window.*] Can't you let a man even *die* in peace?

> *George valiantly struggles to his feet, walks to the door, and slowly opens it. A woman in her forties, followed by a younger man, enter the room. Both are dressed in business attire. The younger man carries an attaché case.*

Becky   Took a while there, George?

> *George closes door. He turns to face the couple, who are now in middle of room inspecting their surroundings, and then walks back to armchair and sits.*

George   What do you two want? [*Distantly*] Who's George…?

Becky   You invited us. Don't you remember?

George   No… I… I haven't been myself lately.

Jonathon   [*as though talking to a child*] Your fifth novel, George. A Strange Affair. You've spent five years of your life writing it. Becky and I are here to view your work. [*To Becky*] I'm not sure that he quite remembers us.

George   I remember you. You're my publisher. [*To Becky*] And my agent. I just don't

remember inviting you here. It's finished. It's on the desk over there. You can take

your pound of flesh and then leave me alone with my thoughts.

Becky walks to the writing desk and picks up manuscript and starts to read.

Becky   You had us worried. When you missed the deadline… Jonathon and I were concerned.

For a long time. It's not like you. You're usually so… *reliable.*

George   I struggled. For some reason this was the hardest book I've ever had to write. Usually

the words come to me. But the voices and words in my head seem to have become

fainter. Less pronounced. I think I may be losing my creative ability. I'm not sure I've

any more books left in me. I feel confused. Depleted.

Jonathon   All good writers think the same. You're one of our bestsellers, George. We wouldn't

want to lose you. You've always been up there with the best of them.

Becky   Tell us about your book, George. Where did you get the idea for your characters?

George   They were all based on people I met. Many years ago. When I was so very young. I can

picture them all now. Like it was yesterday. I've used them in every book.

Becky   I remember your synopsis. From all that time ago. After you finished your last book

The Shepherd's Revolt.

George   It's a tale beyond tragedy. Betrayal. Deception. Guilt. Seems to be a recurring theme in

all of my books.

Becky   Why do you think that is?

George   [*distant*] Something that happened. Long ago. Somewhere deep in my past.

Jonathon   What happened? Can you remember?

George	I've tried to remember but I seem to have blocked it out. It's like it was plucked from my brain. Sometimes I can picture things from the past, but there's a gap. It's just a blur. I must be getting old or something. It's quite frightening you know not being able to remember things. I'm not quite sure what's going on anymore. It's as if somebody has removed the part of my brain that's supposed to remember these things. I suppose it happens to all of us. In the end.
Jonathon	It's all that booze you've been putting away. Place even smells like a brewery.
Becky	Been overcooking the goose, George.
George	I'm an alcoholic. [*Looks Becky in the eye*] It's what we do.
Jonathon	I never know why writers often feel the need to take to the bottle.
George	Because it takes us to a different place. Enables us to forget about ourselves. We're able to inhabit a different world. For a while. Gives us the freedom to write of other things besides our own limited existence.
Jonathon	In a place that is unreal?
George	I have a slender grip on reality these days.
Becky	Are you ready, George?
George	[*sleepy*] Hmm?
Jonathon	[*to Becky*] Look at this place. It's like walking into a scene from his book.
Becky	It does have a certain charm to it.
Jonathon	Bit like George. [*Looks at George*] Think he's in a different place.
Becky	Never judge a book by its cover, Jonathon. The man's a genius. While working on his previous book he spent a year in a remote Welsh cottage.

Jonathon   A sort of method writer? That explains a lot. Certainly all of this.

George   I was in love with her, you know.

Becky   I didn't know that, George.

George   It was such a long time ago. In a faraway place. Vague memories. So distant.

Jonathon   Are you ready, George?

George   Hmm?

Becky   You were saying you were in love?

George   I was very young. I felt things for her that young men weren't supposed to feel. It took over my very being. You see, I hadn't known love before. Didn't know what it was. Being an orphan one feels… *conditioned*. Unloved. But this was so… *intense*. Entirely one sided, of course. But it felt like nothing I'd ever felt before. Or since. It was as if I was gripped by an overwhelming feeling of… belonging. Nothing else seemed to be of any significance whatsoever. I suppose I'd always hoped that I would feel that same immeasurable feeling again, but it always ended badly.

Becky   In what way?

Jonathon and Becky begin to pick up the glasses and bottles and walk to the kitchen. Bars are now seen on the window as the light begins to fade. Moonlight shines on George as darkness eclipses the surrounding area giving the impression of a much narrower room.

George   Expectations never quite realised. Nothing ever seeming to be quite what it should be. Even love. It's odd. I've written five books and in each of them a woman dies.

Jonathon and Becky return from the kitchen. Each are now wearing white lab coats. Becky has a syringe in her hand.

Becky   Are you ready, George?

George holds out his arm instinctively and rolls up his sleeve. His body rocks slowly back and forth.

George   I've often asked myself why did they have to die? It doesn't make sense. Nothing makes sense to me anymore.

Becky administers the medication, while Jonathon holds George steady.

Jonathon   It's because you still haven't come to terms with what you did, George. The novels you write are all in your head. We've *talked* about this. The characters are people you met when you were young. During troubled times. It's your way of distancing yourself from the reality of what happened. All those years ago. You're sick. Delusional. That's why you're here. We're here to help you through this.

Becky   You're safe here George. Others are safer for you being here.

George   [*now mellow*] Safe... Yes… Safe… [*Becky and Jonathon exit the room. George slowly rocks back and forth*] They thought I killed her. They convinced *me* that I did. I *believed* them. For such a long time. But why would I *do* that? It no longer makes sense. I *loved* her. With all my heart. Never knew such love. Before or since. Real love. Love that burns. Inside. Touched my soul. [*Pause*] Images... Flickering. [*We see at the window a brief image of George and his ex-teacher, in the classroom, in an embrace during the zeppelin bombardment*] After all this time. [*Look of fear in George's eyes*] The voices. They're back. Oh god... They want me to write again. To continue with this madness.

George stands and walks about the room as though trying to decipher where the voices are coming from.

Voices   [*echoing and repeated until all voices speak at the same time*] It was a day that seemed to be without end. He looked through the window like a man possessed. Searching as though for his very soul. Each day began the same. Somewhere out there in the darkness lay the answer. Hidden behind stormy clouds perhaps a grain of truth? A key to unlock the mystery. A reality beyond imagination. He was on a journey without end.

George holds his hands over his ears.

George   [*screams*] NO. [*The voices fade into silence*] I *didn't* kill her. She killed her*self.* [*We see a brief image at the window of George's ex-teacher hanging from a rope*] I remember… I untied the rope. As best I could. Too awful to contemplate. Unspeakable. She was already lifeless. Ran away from there. Fast. They arrested me. After I attended the funeral. Kept me isolated. Shock treatment. [*At the window we briefly see George lying on a bed with his head wired up, with a leather mouth guard clenched between his teeth as he is administered electric shocks*] Medication. For all those years. Couldn't tell them what happened. Too… *troubled.* Unable to talk to them. That's when I really listened to the voices. When they first started to write the novels. This is the first time that the voices are silenced. Perhaps this is what redemption feels like? The fulfilment of a long journey through hell. The release of torment. Like rats leaving a sinking ship. The final chapter... of a strange affair.

George can see the image of the schoolboy at the window, and they look at each other. The boy smiles, turns, and is seen walking away. The vision fades.

Lights fade.

Play ends.

The Folly

A Moment in Time

A five act play

Written by **Colin Fantham**

ISBN: 9798355105235

CHARACTERS

The Hathertons

Father	MAXWELL
Mother	CONSTANCE
Daughter	GRACE
Daughter	PRUDENCE
Daughter	CORDELIA
Son	EDGAR
Daughter	GRACE (in later life)

The Buckleys

Father	WILFRED
Son	FELIX
Son	ALBERT
Family friend	CLAUDE DENNING

PROLOGUE

Albert's room, stage left. Albert sits at his candlelit desk, writing frantically. He is a dishevelled long haired man in his forties who looks older than his age, dressed in dark formal Victorian clothes that have seen better days. Although unkempt, he retains a sharp sense of character and purpose. A half-emptied decanter of spirits sits upon the desk with an empty glass beside it. He occasionally dips his pen into a pot of ink to replenish its lifeblood, and continues on in his quest.

After a prolonged period of endeavour, Albert puts down his pen and looks to the heavens briefly as if seeking redemption for his efforts. He pours some of the spirits into the glass and downs it in one. Having replaced the decanter and glass he then addresses the audience as though confronting his internal demons.

Albert   The scene has now been set on this perilous journey into my past and the past of others that remain dear to me. Such tales that were born from a chance encounter within that place of enchantment long ago... Who would have believed that these dark and unearthly events could have sprung from such a glorious beginning? That I, Albert Buckley, could have been so touched with love and despair in equal measure, to commit ink to paper. And yet they are as real to me as the very air I breathe. [*Pause*] I seek not to persuade the unenlightened of my deathly and spiritual imaginings, but merely to reflect the reality that burns within my torn soul from past experience. Loves and lives lost through cruel circumstance, extinguished as a candle from the hand of a broken man. [*Pause*] If it was but a dream, I would have dismissed it from my mind as surely as a tree discards its leaves in the midst of autumn... it would have been kind relief. It is the essence of reality that has been my unmaking. It has made me who I am... and reflects who I was. [*Pause*] It is said by others that love has the ability to overcome great adversity... but it also has the propensity to break hearts and minds with its unwavering attachment; a condition of which I am only too familiar. But from where did this story live until its last faltering breath? [*Pause*] It was within a place of enchantment, remote and long since withered from neglect and antiquity. But it had a substance far beyond the meaning of mere words; and far beyond that of a mortal world…

Albert extinguishes the candle.

Lights fade.

ACT ONE

Soulful music.

The enchanted area. A dense wooded area packed with tall trees, wild plants, and late summer foliage. Birdsong and the sound of nature's creatures can occasionally be heard. Stage right of centre within this enchantment lies the folly. The folly is an ornate white stoned circular construction with two imposing pillars on each side of the wide entrance, above which is a latticed domed roof; a simple seating platform is attached to its lower outer perimeter; a stone statue of a winged angel playing a small harp stands regally beside the few steps that lead up to the centre; there are also steps at the rear, unseen. In the centre of the folly are two adjacent plain stone seats. Left of centre is a cast iron rustic bench painted white. Sunlight can be seen encroaching from on high between plant life and directly upon the middle of the setting.

> *Grace enters stage right shortly followed by Edgar. Grace holds a sketch pad and pencil. Edgar holds a small hamper and a long stick that he has found on his travels. Grace looks to the folly in awe.*

Grace   Oh, how beautiful. Look Edgar. Have you ever seen anything so enchanting?

Edgar   It is rather grand.

Grace   And in such a setting... I shall simply have to draw it.

> *Grace sits cross legged on the ground before the folly and begins her sketch.*

Edgar   Must you draw everything that you see?

Grace   Of course. How else will we remember where we've been and what we've seen when we're old and grey? It is a moment in time that will last forever.

> *An unexpected gust of wind invades the air.*

Edgar   [*looks about him*] A moment in time…You are funny Grace. I intend never to be old and

grey. I shall stay forever young. [*Puts hamper down and adopts a knight's pose with his

stick*] I am King Arthur's knight of the round table. Sir Lancelot. Have at thee foul knight.

Edgar swishes his stick and is busy slaying imaginary foes with great gusto. Prudence

and Cordelia enter from left. Cordelia holds a parasol above her head.

Cordelia   Really you two. Running off like a pair of rough stallions. It's a wonder we didn't lose

you. Mother was sick with worry. As if she doesn't have enough to contend with.

Prudence admires her surroundings.

Prudence   Oh look Cordelia. Such beauty.

Cordelia   It is very pretty here.

Prudence   Pretty? Why, it's breath-taking. One can almost imagine fairies peering out at us from

beneath the leaves. Do you not think so?

Cordelia   Such an imagination you have Prudence. [*Looks around her*] More likely to be robbers

and ne'er-do-wells. As always you have your head in the clouds. [*Unfurls her parasol*]

It's all those silly books that you read. I do believe they've turned your mind to mush.

Grace   I think it's heavenly. How can anyone think otherwise?

Maxwell and his wife Constance enter from right. Maxwell supports himself with a

walking cane. Constance walks beside her husband arm in arm; she holds her parasol

above her head.

Maxwell   [*slightly breathless*] We must have walked many a mile. I must say we deserve a

reprieve. [*Looks around him*] Such splendid isolation.

Maxwell sits at the edge of the folly and mops his brow with a handkerchief.

Constance Are you alright my dear? You look tired. Perhaps we should venture back?

Maxwell   I'll have none of it. We'll rest a while. Enjoy our surroundings. It's not every day you see

a folly as majestic as this one.

Edgar   A folly? I thought that meant nonsense, father?

Maxwell   I suppose it does. It also means a building without purpose.

Cordelia   Well that is a nonsense. How can a building not have a purpose?

Maxwell   When it is of no discernible use but is nonetheless pleasing to the eye.

Prudence   Then surely that *is* its purpose?

Maxwell   [*unsure*] Well… Err…Yes… But…Err…You see…

Constance   Don't badger your father, children.

Grace   It's such a splendid thing. It's rather like a stage. And we're the audience waiting for the

performance. I wonder what it shall be?

Prudence   A Roman tragedy perhaps?

Edgar enters the folly eagerly and faces his audience, brandishing his stick.

Edgar   Yes. Coriolanus. "Hail, Lords! I am return'd your soldier, no more infected with my

country's love than when I parted hence, but still subsisting under your great command"

Maxwell   Well said, oh noble knight.

Edgar   I'm afraid that's the only part that I can remember.

Edgar steps down from the folly.

Constance   It was said with great countenance, Edgar.

Edgar   It's odd. Before I entered the folly, I'd forgotten all about Coriolanus. For a moment I

felt I *was* Coriolanus.

Grace   Perhaps the folly has mystic qualities?

Cordelia   You're as fanciful as Prudence. I imagine *you'll* be seeing fairies at every turn before long.

Prudence   Must you be such an irritation? Just because you're the eldest doesn't mean you have to be so *mean* to everybody.

Constance   [*to Prudence*] With age comes responsibility. [*Unfurls parasol*] It's our duty to be as practical and supportive as we are able. [*To Cordelia*] But we must be civilised in our attitude to others. Especially when they are members of one's own family.

Cordelia   [*contrite*] Yes mother.

Constance   [*to Grace*] Do please stand up child. Your dress will be a crumpled mess.

Grace duly stands but continues to sketch the folly in earnest.

Grace   Yes mother.

Maxwell   It occurs to me that we are much in need of refreshment. All this walking has given me a thirst. [*To Edgar*] The hamper if you will.

Edgar   Yes father.

Edgar dutifully passes the hamper to his father. Maxwell proceeds to pass each of the family a glass and then takes the stopper from a bottle of lemonade and begins equally distributing it into each glass.

Prudence   Such a treat to have fresh lemonade.

Cordelia   On such a day as this. Glorious.

Grace   A day that will be forever with us.

Edgar   A day unlike any other, I believe.

Constance   Yes. It is rather splendid here. I feel such a calm spirit in the air. It feels almost as if

somehow I had been here before. But I know I have not.

Prudence   Perhaps you were here in your dreams?

Cordelia   That sounds rather fanciful? Even for you Prudence. It is a physical impossibility to

inhabit one's dreams.

Prudence   In the spiritual world who knows what is possible and what is not?

Maxwell   [*raises glass*] May I propose a toast? To her Majesty the Queen.

They each raise their glass.

All   The Queen.

As each begin drinking, Wilfred Buckley enters far left, followed by Albert,
Felix and Claude.

Wilfred   [*to Maxwell*] I hope we're not intruding? We were out walking and found ourselves

drawn like a magnet to this magnificent structure.

Grace   It's a folly.

Wilfred   Is it, by jove?

Edgar   A building without purpose.

Wilfred   I do believe that you are correct.

Prudence   Although pleasing to the eye.

Wilfred   It certainly is, isn't it?

Cordelia   Which would *be* its purpose.

Wilfred   [*puzzled*] You know… I suppose it would.

Constance   [*slightly flustered*] Thank you children.

Maxwell   [*now standing*] Where are my manners? [*Offers hand to Wilfred who shakes it heartily*] Maxwell Hatherton. And this is my wife, Constance.

Constance   I'm pleased to meet you Mr...?

Wilfred   Buckley. [*Offers hand to Constance who receives it warmly*] Wilfred Buckley.

Maxwell   [*gestures to his children*] These are our children: Edgar, Cordelia, Prudence and Grace.

Wilfred   Charming. [*Turns to his party*] These are my two sons Albert and Felix with their good friend Claude.

Albert   [*to Cordelia*] It's quite a gathering isn't it? I hope we're not too much of an encumbrance to you all.

Cordelia   It's always good to make new acquaintances, Mr Buckley.

Albert   Please. Call me Albert.

Felix   [*to Grace*] Are you a competent artist, Grace? [*Gestures to sketch pad*] May I see?

Grace   [*reluctantly shows her picture*] It's not a very good likeness, I'm afraid. I'm not sure I've captured its beauty as well as I should have.

Felix   Oh, but it's wonderful. You have the essence of it for sure. It's quite magical. I almost feel that I could just walk right into the page.

Grace   [*smiling widely*] Praise indeed.

Claude   [*to Prudence*] Tell me Prudence, are you the recipient of a special talent?

Prudence   None whatsoever I'm ashamed to say. I'm told I'm a terrible bookworm. My elder sister teases me endlessly. Presently I am reading Alice's Adventures in Wonderland.

Claude   A splendid read. Quite fantastical.

Prudence   [*laughs*] Is there such a word?

Claude   Lewis Carroll is quite the genius. Misunderstood perhaps?

Prudence   Indeed. Such a creative spirit, don't you think?

Claude   Without question.

Constance   [*to Wilfred*] It's a pity your good lady wife isn't here to join us, Mr Buckley?

Wilfred   [*downcast*] Yes. [*Hesitates*] I am a widower. She died several years ago.

Constance   I am so sorry. I had no idea. How foolish of me.

Wilfred   [*recovered*] Not at all. How could you know? Do call me Wilfred.

Constance   [*uncertain*] Wilfred.

Maxwell   Would you like to join us in a glass of lemonade? We have another bottle.

Wilfred   [*politely dismissive*] We wouldn't want to inconvenience you.

Maxwell   I won't hear of it. Although I am afraid we only have the six glasses.

Maxwell takes out bottle and removes stopper.

Constance   Mr Buckley can have mine. [*Offers empty glass*] I've finished.

Wilfred   I couldn't possibly.

Constance   I insist.

Wilfred   Then I shall have to accept. [*Takes glass and bows his head slightly*] You're very kind. Constance.

Cordelia   [*offering her glass*] Albert, you must have mine.

Albert   This is very irregular.

Cordelia   I insist.

Albert   [*takes glass reluctantly*] Then I too must accept. With due humility. And gratitude.

> *Maxwell begins pouring lemonade into each glass.*

Prudence   [*offers glass*] Claude can have mine.

Claude   [*takes glass*] How refreshing. I accept your kind offer, Prudence.

Grace   [*offering glass to Felix*] I'd be disheartened if you didn't accept my glass Felix.

Felix   [*accepting glass*] I would never wish to dishearten you Grace. [*Takes glass*] You're very kind, I'm sure.

Wilfred   [*raises glass and glances at each of the Hathertons*] Your very good health.

> *Albert, Claude and Felix also raise their glass. Each takes a drink.*

Maxwell   And to you all. Sad to say *my* health has seen rather better days.

Wilfred   I'm so sorry. You look the very picture of robust health.

Maxwell   It's my breathing. It is in decline. Not all it's supposed to be, I'm afraid. I'm not as young as I once was. One takes one's health for granted when one is young, of course, which is the way of things. But when you reach a certain vintage… you realise how fragile life can be.

Wilfred   Undoubtedly so.

Constance Doctor Hendry insists Maxwell take frequent long walks in the fresh air.

Wilfred   Sage advice indeed. [*To Maxwell*] I'm sure your malaise will be a temporary inconvenience to you.

Maxwell   I'm hoping to retire by the coast. Perhaps Brighton? I'm told the air there has a purity all of its own.

Wilfred   Indeed. Quite bracing. May I ask what line of work you are in?

Maxwell   Textiles. It's a small concern. But the demand is growing thanks to improved methods

of manufacture, although there are now many other factories trading also in the area. I'm

hoping that Edgar will assume control when he is of age.

Edgar   Must I father? I would much sooner be a great explorer in Africa, such as David

Livingstone. Such adventures to be had. Such sights to be seen. Exploring the

unexplored and seeing the world.

Wilfred   A noble quest indeed. You have much spirit, Edgar. But I fancy your father has great need

of your endeavours. I'm sure there will be time enough for you to see the world.

The Buckleys return their empty glasses to the hamper.

Edgar   [*reluctantly*] I suppose you're right.

Constance [*to Wilfred*] And what line of work are you in, Mr Buckley?

Wilfred   Do please call me Wilfred. I have the very good fortune to be retired these last five years.

I have had the distinction of serving in her Majesty's armed forces for nigh on thirty

years.

Edgar   So you must have seen some action during the Crimean war?

Wilfred   [*subdued*] Indeed I did. I was at the Siege of Sevastopol.

Felix stands before Grace who busily sketches his portrait.

Edgar   [*enthusiastically*] That must have been dreadfully exciting. Did you kill many Russians?

Constance [*aghast*] You must excuse Edgar. He is so terribly young.

Wilfred   Ah, the exuberance of youth. There is nothing to be excused. It is nature's way of things. I

too was young and fresh faced when I first joined her Majesty's army. It's only when you experience the reality of war… [*Sadness etched in his eyes*] But one mustn't dwell on

life's misgivings. It is far too short, is it not?

Albert   Father was awarded the Victoria Cross for bravery in the field of battle.

Prudence How splendid.

Constance [*to Wilfred*] You must be terribly proud?

Wilfred   It *is* a great honour. [*Poignant*] But I would gladly have exchanged it for the lives of my

fallen comrades.

Maxwell   [*serious*] We owe a debt of gratitude to you and your kind. The Empire's future is a

happy one because of your noble contribution.

Wilfred   A minor one I assure you, compared to others.

Constance [*to Albert and Claude*] And what of you fine young men? What will become of

you, I wonder?

Albert   Quite a dull affair, I'm afraid. Claude and I attend Winchester College. We spend long

hours reciting Latin and pondering mathematical equations.

Claude   Days that seem to last an eternity, I assure you.

Prudence It sounds divine. Such a fine place of learning. [*Slightly irritated*] You are lucky.

Maxwell   A young gentleman will always benefit from a good understanding of the classics.

Claude   I intend to join the banking profession when I leave. If it will have me. Although I'm not

terribly good at mathematics. Unlike Albert, who is a natural at *everything*. Especially

sports. I'm Harry Hopeless compared to Albert.

Albert   Claude is being his usual modest self. He is perfectly capable when it comes to all aspects

of self-improvement.

Cordelia   And what of your aspirations, Albert? What do *you* hope to achieve in life?

Albert   [*slightly embarrassed*] You will think me a light hearted fool.

Cordelia   [*serious*] I would never think that of you, I assure you. Ever.

Albert   I have pretensions to be a writer. Of plays. For the theatre. [*Relieved*] There. I have said it.

Cordelia   But I think that is a wonderful ambition.

Wilfred   [*dismissive*] It is not a reputable profession for a young gentleman. The theatre? [*Looks heavenwards*] No. You know that I heartily disapprove. [*Looks to Albert*] You shall be something in the City. A man with your abilities… why, he can have the world in the palm of his hands. [*Holds out his hand*] In the palm of his hands, sir.

Albert   Perhaps I could be both a something in the City, *and* a writer of plays, father?

Pause.

Wilfred   [*quietly resigned*] Perhaps...

Grace   Surely if Albert followed in the footsteps of the famous William Shakespeare, it would be a very noble path indeed to take?

Claude   Well said Grace. I have read some of Albert's work and I have no doubt there is a quality that would not be out of place in the finest theatres of our age.

Constance   [*to Wilfred*] I seem to be the cause of some consternation. It was not my intention. Please forgive me.

Wilfred   Not at all. I *am* a very proud father. I just want the best for Albert. As I do Felix. The future can be a dark and forlorn place without due regard. The theatre is looked upon as a somewhat frivolous occupation in some quarters of society.

Edgar   [*outraged*] Then society is a blithering fool.

Cordelia   [*horrified*] EDGAR. Keep a civil tongue in your head. [*Uncomfortable*] Most

unbefitting.

Edgar   [*to others*] I'm sorry. But society must be very stupid if it thinks the theatre is of little

consequence. Why, it's the very *height* of a civilised society.

Maxwell   [*to Wilfred*] You must excuse Edgar. He has a spirit sometimes unbecoming for his age.

Wilfred   Consider it of no matter. Edgar's spirit is infectious even if it is a trifle misplaced. [*To

Edgar] You see… there are elements of theatre that are not serious endeavours and bring

it into disrepute. But you are far too young to be aware of those.

Prudence   Are the disreputable performances ones that *you* have encountered Mr Buckley?

Wilfred   [*caught unawares*] Well … I… you see… Err…

Constance   [*embarrassed*] Prudence. That is not a question suitable for a young lady to ask a

gentleman. [*To Wilfred*] I am so sorry.

Prudence   [*innocently*] I didn't mean any offence, Mr Buckley.

Wilfred   Quite alright. It seems I am the one who should apologise. [*Looks to Albert*] You *are* a

gifted writer Albert, it is true, and I hope for success in all that you achieve. But you

must be mindful that very few writers of note find fame and fortune. That is all I ask.

Albert   Yes father. I will take your advice to heart.

Claude   [*looks to others*] Then all is well. This is indeed a happy day.

Grace   [*still drawing Felix*] It's the enchantment of the folly. Can't you feel it?

Felix   The folly, Grace?

Grace   Oh yes. I'm quite decided that it has a spirit all of its own. Perhaps a healing spirit?

Felix   How could it possibly? It is an inanimate object after all. It has no sense. Therefore it cannot think, eat, or breathe. How could it possibly heal if it hasn't even been to medical college?

Laughter from the others.

Maxwell   [*still laughing*] Well said, young man. Well said.

Edgar   [*now standing on the base of the folly and leaning out*] Perhaps the folly is just a figment of our imagination? And we are all ghosts drawn like a river to the sea?

Wilfred   [*smiling*] Quite a fanciful notion. Eloquently put. But we are all quite real I assure you Edgar.

Edgar   [*uncomfortable*] It's strange. I suddenly felt a chill run through me.

Maxwell   No more talk of ghosts, Edgar. You have given yourself a fright, that is all.

Prudence   Well I for one think that Grace is correct in her imagining. Who are we to say otherwise when there are so many mysteries in life?

Cordelia   [*cynical*] It is a mystery that will be forever lost on me, I do believe.

Albert   [*resolutely*] Then you must be healed, Cordelia. Forthwith.

Albert moves to the foot of the steps to the folly and beckons Cordelia with his outstretched arm.

Cordelia   [*looks on in disbelief*] I do believe you have lost all reason, Albert.

Albert   I believe you are quite correct. But nonetheless do please join me because I suddenly feel quite extravagantly foolish.

Cordelia looks to her mother for guidance.

Cordelia   [*unsure*] Mother?

Constance [*lightly*] Who are we to deny the power of the folly?

Cordelia [*to Albert*] Then I shall join you but only to appease your feelings of foolish guilt.

Cordelia walks to Albert and accepts his hand. They walk up the steps of the folly and amble around its interior, side by side. They stop between two pillars and silently look out at their surroundings immersed in each other's presence. The others look on in bemused contemplation. Claude summons up the courage to stand at the foot of the folly, beckoning with outstretched arm for Prudence to join him.

Claude May I escort you to the folly, Prudence?

Prudence Well... I'm sure it would be churlish of me to refuse such a kind offer, Claude.

Prudence looks to her father who nods his consent. Prudence accepts Claude's hand, and they too enter the folly. Felix follows the precedent set and duly stands at the foot of the folly with outstretched arm, appealing to Grace to accompany him.

Felix [*flamboyantly*] Grace... will you do me the very great honour of joining me?

Grace Oh yes. [*A cough from her father. Grace turns to him*] With your permission of course, father?

Maxwell [*warmly*] Granted, my dearest young Grace.

Grace accepts Felix's hand, and they enter the folly.

Wilfred [*looks to Constance and signals with his hand towards the folly*] With Maxwell's permission...?

Constance [*alarmed*] Most irregular.

Maxwell [*lightly waves them on*] You have not only my permission sir, but my blessing also.

Constance [*to Wilfred*] Are you quite sure, my dear?

Maxwell   Quite sure. [*Sits at the edge of the folly and wipes his forehead with his handkerchief*] I

intend to sit here and rest a while.

Constance   [*pleasantly bemused*] Then with my husband's consent I feel inclined to accept your kind

invitation.

Constance joins Wilfred and they walk slowly up the steps together, side by side, to the

folly. Maxwell looks to the heavens and gives a sentimental knowing smile.

Lights fade.

Albert's room. Faint daylight. Albert continues to write.

After a while he rises, drink in hand, walks to window and peers out, in contemplative

mood. He takes out his pocket watch and views the time; he returns it to his pocket, and

then turns to audience.

Albert   Time… It is ever-present and formidable in its relentless execution. It is the warm

bringer of life… and the cold harbinger of death. Within five years' passing, Edgar had

succumbed to the ravages of fever that had dispatched so many others in its sorry wake.

Destined to remain forever young. His life unfulfilled. Such a cruel circumstance…

Maxwell Hatherton lapsed shortly thereafter from weakness of the lungs and, it is said, a

heaviness of the heart. Though long since passed, their spirits, as within us all, lived on.

As if pulled by a celestial hand, they endured within the enchanted area of the folly - a

moment of transition before their journey to a better place. [*Long pause*] Fortune

favoured a new alliance between my father and Constance. A match fused with love

and practicality, but tinged with the sorrow and hardship that loss of economic

prosperity brings…

Lights fade.

ACT TWO

Soulful music.

The enchanted area. Late summer. The folly now has some ivy growing around the pillars and along its dome. The statue is more weathered than it once was.

> *Constance and Wilfred enter from left. Constance walks beside Wilfred, arm in arm; she holds a parasol above her head. Their attire is more formal and less colourful than previously seen. Maxwell sits at the right edge of the folly. Edgar leans between two pillars on the left of the folly, looking out. Maxwell and Edgar's appearance and attire are the same as they were previously.*

Constance Look Wilfred. We are here.

Wilfred Ah, the folly. It is like seeing an old friend, is it not?

Constance An old friend who has aged slightly. As have we.

> *Constance breaks from Wilfred and unfurls her parasol.*

Wilfred Such is the way of things. With time's passing.

Constance And yet it is still somehow… majestic. It has been quite a while, has it not?

Wilfred [*nodding*] A good while.

Constance Yes. [*Reflective*] So much has happened since then.

Wilfred Good and bad.

Constance [*distant*] Good and *bad* indeed.

Wilfred We mustn't dwell on life's… misfortunes. We must look to the future. I believe it is what Maxwell would have wanted.

Constance Poor Maxwell. He worked so hard. And to what end?

Wilfred [*to himself*] To his *own* end, I fear.

Constance   And my son. [*Voice quivering with emotion*] Oh Wilfred. Life can be so wretched. He was just a boy.

Wilfred   I have seen death many times in the field of battle, but Edgar's cruel passing at such a young age… [*Emotional*] He was a fine boy. Such spirit. His time unmercifully cut short.

Constance sits at the bench, disconsolate.

Constance   I have tried to find sense in it all. But there is none.

Wilfred   We can at least console ourselves that his suffering was not prolonged. The fever was indeed swift in its delivery.

Constance   I had such hopes for his future. [*Pause*] And now he is gone. My darling boy.

Wilfred   We *must* be strong… Mrs Buckley.

Constance wipes a tear from her eye.

Constance   Yes.

Wilfred consoles his wife.

Edgar   Can they not see us, father?

Maxwell   No. It is the way of things. Be not afraid Edgar.

Edgar   I am not afraid. I'm strangely at peace with the world. But it pains me seeing Mother so distressed.

Edgar blows a kiss in her direction. Constance looks up from her despair, touches her cheek with her hand and smiles at Wilfred

Wilfred   [*to Constance*] That's the spirit.

Maxwell and Edgar smile to each other.

Constance   [*composing herself*] I'd forgotten quite how tranquil it was here. [*Looks around her*] It's almost comforting, despite everything. So peaceful.

Wilfred   Yes. It is rather splendid. One can quite forget the travails of life in such a setting.

Reflective pause.

Constance   You have always shown a strength of character, despite adversity.

Wilfred   Probably my army training. It has overcome many an obstacle in life.

Constance   And yet it occurs to me that you have never shared with me your experience of life during your war years?

Wilfred   [*serious*] Nor will I, my dear. It is certainly not for the ear of a lady. [*Dismissive*] Think nothing of such things.

Constance   You sleep so little. Your mind is… *troubled*. I am woken often by the sound of your discomfort during the early hours.

Wilfred   It is only in the dead of night that the devils seem to dance within me.

Edgar   Can we not help Wilfred with his demons?

Maxwell   We must encourage him to speak of his experience lest I fear his torment will be forever with him.

Maxwell stands beside Wilfred.

Constance   And these devils that dance within you… what form do they take?

Maxwell gently pats Wilfred on the back.

Maxwell   Be not afraid dear friend. Open up your sorrow.

Wilfred   [*looks distantly ahead*] The many pale faces of death.

Constance And do you recognise those pale faces?

Wilfred nods in sorrowful reflection.

Wilfred They are the faces of comrades who were dispatched by the enemy… and the faces of those killed through my actions. Each fighting for a cause they believed in. In my dreams I can see them all as they fell. Their faces and bodies contorted with the horror of death. Some almost unrecognisable through violence and dismemberment. Shadows of their former selves. Hollow and void of life. Such tragic waste of humanity...

Edgar I feel a cloud has been lifted from Wilfred's heart.

Maxwell Indeed so.

Constance We are husband and wife. We must share life's concerns.

Wilfred You are right. I see now it is well to share such things.

Constance Poor Wilfred. [*Pause*] You have taken on much by marrying me.

Wilfred [*earnest*] If I had my time again it would not be otherwise, I assure you.

Constance But to inherit such debts…

Wilfred [*dismissive*] A small price to pay.

Maxwell [*shakes head*] True to say I was not an astute businessman.

Edgar Are they now poor, father?

Maxwell I fear that they are not as affluent as they once were, for sure.

Constance It seems so unfair. That you be financially burdened through marriage.

Maxwell A cruel fate. Most undeserved.

Wilfred I still have a small pension which will sustain us in our hour of need.

Constance   But to be obliged to sell the family business. To lose one's standing in society… One's

property. [*Looks blankly ahead*] Our children forced to live elsewhere with our relatives.

What is to become of us?

Wilfred   [*comforting*] We will live a life as best we can.

Maxwell   Well said, Wilfred.

Constance   And what of our children?

Wilfred   They will fare as best as they are able. They have had a good start in life. It is for them to

make the most of it.

Constance   They are all so close.

Wilfred   Our matrimony has made them closer still.

Constance   Brothers and sisters in spirit and in law.

Edgar   Brothers. [*Animated*] I have *brothers,* father.

Maxwell   Indeed you have Edgar. In spirit and in law. For now, and forever.

Edgar   Imagine that. I love my sisters dearly, but I always wanted a brother. [*Serious*] And now

I have *two.*

Maxwell   Indeed you have. I am happy for you.

Wilfred   They are each now of an age and will find their own way in the world, I am sure.

Constance   But it is such an uncertain world, Wilfred. I fear for their futures.

Wilfred   It is mostly out of our hands now, my dear. We must have faith that they will tread the

right path.

Constance   Grace has such notions to be an artist.

Wilfred   And so she should. I have seen her work. Most agreeable. She is well equipped to be

something in the art world I wouldn't wonder.

Maxwell   Dearest Grace. Such a spirit of endeavour. It wouldn't surprise me in the least.

Edgar   Perhaps she will exhibit her work one day?

Maxwell   You know, I am most certain she will.

Constance   And yet it is so difficult for a female artist to be recognised for her talent. One has only

to read *The Tenant of Wildfell Hall* to be reminded of how precarious the nature of a

woman's artistic ambitions can be.

Wilfred   As we approach a new century, I am sure the present attitude of many a man will cease

to be a burden upon the shoulders of a talented woman such as Grace.

Constance   I only hope that you are right. [*Pause*] And Cordelia? What will become of our eldest

daughter?

Maxwell   Ah Cordelia. A firm head on her shoulders, that one.

Wilfred   I am afraid that she is much taken with Albert. A match that cannot blossom because

of our own wedlock. Why, in the eyes of the law... No. We must prevent their attachment

at all costs.

Constance   But how can we prevent love, Wilfred? It is such a powerful force.

Wilfred paces up and down deep in thought. Maxwell paces up and down beside Wilfred.

Maxwell   Indeed it is.

Edgar   How can love be a bad thing, father? Surely it is a thing for good?

Maxwell   [*stops pacing and turns to Edgar*] Ordinarily yes. But I fear that in the other world there

are practical and moral rules that prevent it.

Wilfred   Perhaps we can send her away?

Constance Surely there must be a better solution?

Wilfred   [*Ponders deeply*] You have a sister in Canterbury.

Constance But that is so very far. [*Exasperated*] She may as well be on the moon.

Wilfred   Then it is decided. She will stay with your sister. It must be arranged.

Constance But on what pretext?

Maxwell   This is indeed a tangled web.

Wilfred   [*considers deeply*] That she is sick and in need of a companion.

Constance My sister is neither sick nor in need of a companion. It will have to be something with at least an element of reality about it.

Wilfred   Hmm.

Wilfred continues to pace up and down with Maxwell by his side doing likewise.

Maxwell   This requires careful consideration.

Wilfred looks as if he has found an answer then dismisses it from his mind.

Edgar   [*in deep thought*] That travel broadens the mind?

Maxwell   Bravo, Edgar.

Wilfred   [*inspired and with conviction*] That travel broadens the mind.

Constance Yes. I believe Cordelia will accept such a proposition.

Wilfred   Strange. I seemed to have plucked that notion out of thin air.

Maxwell   Indeed you did, sir.

Constance   She is young and will find another. In time. [*Pause*] It seems such a cruel twist of

fate.

Maxwell   Cruel indeed.

Edgar   How so Father?

Maxwell   To deny love at such a tender age... It is a bitter pill to swallow.

Edgar   Will Cordelia be much distressed?

Maxwell   [*sad*] I fear so.

Wilfred   We have little choice in the matter.

Maxwell   [*heartfelt*] My poor Cordelia. How I feel for her...

A gust of wind shakes the leaves.

Constance How strange.

Wilfred   My dear?

Constance [*looks to the sky*] The sun burns brightly in the sky and yet... I felt a sudden chill in the

air. Did you not feel it?

Wilfred   [*looks around him*] Mother Nature is indeed a mysterious force. She has a talent to

astonish.

Maxwell   [*gently to Constance*] I didn't mean to startle you, my dear.

Maxwell now stands beside the statue.

Edgar   She cannot hear you, father.

Constance stands and surveys the folly.

Maxwell   [*distantly intense*] There are times when I forget...

Edgar   Do you miss mother, terribly?

Maxwell   Indeed I do, Edgar. *Indeed,* I do. [*Pause*] And yet I am happy that she now has Wilfred. For he is a good man and has my blessing. My love for your mother has not diminished, despite our circumstance. Nor will it ever.

Edgar   My love for her will always shine brightly.

Constance [*turns to Wilfred*] And what of Prudence?

Maxwell   Ah Prudence... Such a delight. Do tell, Wilfred. [*Turns to Edgar*] We are all ears are we not?

Edgar   [*smiling*] We are indeed.

Edgar steps down from the folly and stands still, listening intently.

Wilfred   I believe her future to be an auspicious one.

Maxwell   Praise be.

Constance Agreed. Her engagement to Claude is a happy and fortuitous one.

Wilfred   I am as proud of him as if he were my very own.

Edgar   Hurrah.

In his enthusiasm Edgar has picked a leaf from a nearby plant; Constance witnesses it in awe. Edgar holds the leaf and mimics it swaying in the air and falling to the ground. Constance shakes her head in wonder and then dismisses it from her mind.

Maxwell   Good news indeed.

Constance [*senses now regained*] He has a promising future, I believe?

Wilfred   Indeed he has. He has secured himself a position worthy of a scholar and a gentleman within the London Stock Exchange no less.

Constance A most agreeable occupation.

Wilfred I only wish that Albert had followed him into the financial markets instead of pursuing a literary career in the theatre. But he wouldn't listen. A mule has less stubbornness.

Constance Perhaps in time he will succeed? Others have with lesser talent.

Wilfred I remain unconvinced. It is a bold ambition but how can one survive without regular monetary gain? It can be a cold and heartless world without the necessary finance. I fear he has chosen the wrong path. Because of his weakened mental state, he has also taken to hard liquor. He showed such promise in his academic studies… Instead, he wastes it all on a whim. [*Despairingly*] A whim. I ask you.

Edgar Is it wrong to follow your dreams, father?

Maxwell No. [*Sadly*] It is not wrong. Not wrong at all. I have learned through experience that time is very precious and that dreams should not be denied. But they must be tempered with practical considerations also. Let us hope and pray that Albert is successful in his endeavours.

Edgar I will pray very hard for poor Albert. As I will poor Cordelia.

Maxwell As will I, my boy.

Constance And what will become of Felix?

Maxwell A fine upstanding young man. And quite the wit.

Wilfred He is considering a career in the Royal Navy.

Constance [*exasperated*] Heavens. [*Pause*] He is so young.

Wilfred He is also headstrong. He is quite determined, despite my own misgivings. But he is now old enough to decide his own way in life. I have tried as best I can to illuminate the hardships endured on board ship such as disease and enemy engagement, but his boyish sense of adventure… it has the better of it.

Constance I believe it is a trait that he has inherited from his father.

Wilfred I am afraid it is true. Who am I to deny him the same ambition that fate bestowed upon me?

Constance Then we must support him as best we can in his quest.

Wilfred [*resigned*] That we must.

Maxwell A noble quest indeed. For the good of the empire.

Edgar [*ebullient*] An empire that has the greatest navy in the world.

Maxwell Indeed it has.

Maxwell and Edgar salute each other in their enthusiasm. A sudden clap of thunder is heard; they appear sheepishly guilty for their action.

Constance [*looking above her*] This weather is beyond mystery. Not a cloud in the sky.

Wilfred Perhaps all the smoke from the factory chimneys has affected nature's balance, my dear?

Constance looks to her husband in bewilderment.

Constance [*shakes head*] A quite nonsensical point of view, I believe.

Wilfred Yes... Silly of me. How could it?

Constance Indeed so.

Maxwell We must act with due caution, Edgar, lest our actions betray our… situation.

Edgar Indeed we must. Although there is much excitement and intrigue to be had within our family, is there not?

Maxwell   It is a most beguiling set of circumstances. We must be on our guard to steer our loved

ones through the treacherous oceans of misfortune as best we can.

Edgar   I fear it will not be an easy journey, father.

Maxwell   [*poignant*] It is one that I somehow feel we are obliged to make in order to complete our

own intended passage.

Edgar   [*looks above him*] Yes. I feel it too.

Maxwell   [*serious*] Then it shall be done.

Constance enters the folly as Wilfred looks on. An unexpected gust of wind pervades the

air.

Constance   [*otherworldly*] How strange I feel.

Wilfred   [*concerned*] How so?

Constance looks about her; Maxwell and Edgar stand before the folly and look to her in

earnest.

Constance   You will think me a fool.

Wilfred   I would never think of you as such, I assure you.

Maxwell   Indeed. Nor would I.

Wilfred   What is it, my dear? Are you feeling unwell?

Constance   [*looks to Wilfred*] On the contrary. [*Lightly*] I feel as though I am walking on air.

Wilfred   [*concerned*] Perhaps you should sit for a while? It might clear your head.

Edgar   Is it the enchantment father?

Maxwell   [*hushed tones*] Indeed so, I believe. A powerful force.

Constance [*smiling*] It is a most pleasing affectation. It is as if all the troubles that were once upon

me have been lifted away… by angels.

Wilfred [*sceptical*] Perhaps we should leave?

Constance All is well. And all *will* be well.

Wilfred How say you?

Constance It is not *I* Wilfred.

Wilfred But there *is* only you.

Constance I do not know the words to provide you with a satisfactory answer. I believe there *are*

none. Suffice to say, it is of an order higher than our own.

Maxwell Indeed it is.

Edgar The highest.

Wilfred A most curious development. I am a simple soldier, my dear, but I *have* heard others

speak of such things at the heart of battle. [*Considers hard*] An epiphany I believe they

have called it. I for one have never experienced it and remain sceptical. I believe it to be

an illusion of the mind.

Constance [*holds out her hand*] Then you must join me. Perhaps your scepticism can be cured?

Wilfred considers the invitation.

Edgar Why is he not joining her, father?

Maxwell I believe he is worried of breaking the spell.

Edgar He is a non-believer?

Maxwell He is wary of the unexplained in life and in death.

Constance You hesitate?

Wilfred I would not want you to think ill of me if I do not experience the same euphoria as yourself.

Constance You must put away such notions and accompany me herein. [*Wilfred still hesitates*] You have been in the thick of battle for many a year, and yet feel unable to join me here and now?

Wilfred [*motionless*] I find myself… unable.

Maxwell I feel we must intervene.

Edgar Indeed we must.

Maxwell and Edgar stand either side of the still figure of Wilfred and very lightly touch his shoulder, guiding him towards the folly.

Wilfred [*walking slowly, puppet-like*] A most curious development. It is as though my feet were not my own. It is an astonishing peculiarity, the like of which I have never before encountered.

Constance Why, you are walking as if an infant in its first faltering steps of adventure.

Maxwell and Edgar gently usher Wilfred up the first steps of the folly.

Wilfred [*ecstatic*] I believe you are right, my dear. And it feels just as exhilarating. I feel as though I too am now walking on air. A most welcome sensation has enveloped my entire being. I believe I am drunk with delirium. [*In disbelief*] Why, I feel as tight as a boiled owl.

Wilfred joins his wife within the folly.

Constance You are in earnest, Wilfred? I pray you are not trying to humour me in any way?

Wilfred   I have never been more sincere. I give you the word of an officer and a gentleman

ma'am.

Wilfred salutes his wife in enthusiasm.

Constance Then all is well with the world.

Wilfred   Indeed it is. The world has never looked so clear to me as it does at this very moment.

Wilfred and Constance hold hands as though for the first time; they sit facing each other within the folly, at peace with the world.

Maxwell   A most pleasing sight, is it not?

Edgar   The power of the enchantment has opened their eyes and their hearts.

Maxwell   It is a joyful thing to behold. If their hearts were not true, I feel they would not have experienced such as they have. Their feeling for one another will see them through dark times ahead. [*Thoughtful pause*] They will need that mutual affection. [*Sombre*] Of that I am sadly sure...

Lights fade.

Albert's room. Snow clings to the frosty windowpane. The smouldering embers of a fire cast its presence within the dim light of the room. Albert continues to write.

After a while, Albert rises and stands before the fire, warming his hands. After a period of contemplation, he turns to audience.

Albert   Love's power is like that of a fire. When it is present it fills the soul with warmth and melts even the coldest of hearts. But when it is denied... My attachment to Cordelia was now tainted because of the matrimony between my father and Constance. In the eyes of the law, Cordelia and I were now brother and sister. Our natural bond and destiny forcibly broken by the cruel hand of fate... How strange are the ways of the world... I felt cursed and full with bitterness that torments me still. [*Long pause*] It was to be our last encounter within that place of enchantment, and one that was to have a profound effect upon the rest of our existence in this world… and the next.

Lights fade.

ACT THREE

Soulful music.

The enchanted area. Mid-autumn.

> *Enter Albert and Cordelia from left. Cordelia holds a parasol above her head and walks beside Albert. Maxwell stands by the statue, and Edgar sits on the left edge of the folly looking out.*

Cordelia   [*with finality*] We are here.

> *They stand facing the folly.*

Albert   It feels preordained. [*Pause*] As though the folly had been awaiting our presence. After all these years… A welcome reacquaintance.

> *Maxwell and Edgar look knowingly to each other.*

Cordelia   [*looks about her*] Our first meeting place.

Albert   [*delicately*] And now perhaps our last...

> *Cordelia unfurls her parasol with latent emotion.*

Cordelia   I am told that Canterbury has a rich culture in the arts. I understand it also has a most splendid cathedral. There will be an abundance of news to inform you of, I am sure. I will write every day. And you must tell of all your success as a famous playwright.

Albert   My writing career is proving an onerous one. I presumed my last piece may have fared better. Even Mr Irving at the Lyceum said it had welcome qualities. [*Melancholic*] And yet it lasted but a short season. I am finding life as a writer of plays a most frustrating occupation. My father predicted such an outcome. [*Despondent*] I am beginning to accept his way of thinking.

Cordelia   One day you will write a fine play that will be as worthy as any by Shakespeare. I am certain of it.

Albert   I am not worthy to even stand beneath that great man's shadow. [*Turns to Cordelia*] I have never felt such ineptitude as I have of late.

Maxwell   I feel we must intervene in some way. But I am at a loss...

Edgar   If we could find a way to unburden Albert's despondency…

Maxwell   Yes… But how?

Edgar is in deep thought.

Edgar   Perhaps Albert should write a play about the folly?

Maxwell   [*joyful*] A most splendid proposition.

Maxwell and Edgar look to Albert who now looks at the folly, transfixed.

Cordelia   [*concerned*] Albert?

Albert remains preoccupied. He holds his hand up, weakly, to Cordelia, not wanting to break his train of thought, and continues to be mesmerised. Maxwell walks by the still figure of Albert.

Maxwell   You have given Albert food for thought, Edgar. It is a veritable crumb of comfort in the midst of dejection.

Edgar   A happy interlude, father.

Maxwell   Indeed so.

Albert   [*dazed*] I appear to have been struck by a creative bolt of lightning, Cordelia.

Cordelia   Are you quite alright?

Albert   I am indeed. [*Distant*] Quite alright...

Cordelia   [*to herself*] Writers are a strange breed.

Albert   Hmm?

Cordelia   What have you seen that demands your undivided attention?

Albert   [*incidentally*] I believe I am destined to one day write a play… unlike any other.

Cordelia   Do tell?

Albert   [*gestures extravagantly*] We are within it.

Cordelia   Here and now?

Albert   It is present and all around us.

Cordelia   And what shall you call this great play of yours?

Albert   I shall call it… The Folly.

Cordelia   A simple but fine title.

Albert   [*astounded*] It breathes. I can feel it move within me. There is such drama there. It has

                 restored that within me that was lost.

                 Cordelia turns away to hide her personal sadness.

Cordelia   Divine inspiration has indeed been at play. [*Unconvincingly*] I am happy for you.

Edgar   How can we lighten my sister's heavy heart Father?

Maxwell   I fear we cannot act upon it until chance presents itself.

Edgar   And what if chance fails to present itself?

Maxwell looks to Edgar with sorrow etched upon his face.

Maxwell   Then I fear for them both.

Albert approaches Cordelia and consoles her.

Albert   A most perplexing experience. I- I'm not sure what came over me.

Cordelia   Grace would have said the enchantment. [*Smiles*] Prudence would undoubtedly be of the same mind, I believe.

Albert places his hand upon Cordelia's shoulder.

Albert   My behaviour was uncommonly insensitive. Please don't think ill of me.

Cordelia faces Albert.

Cordelia   How can you think so? There is nothing in my heart but…love. I could never think ill of you. I have felt this way since our first encounter.

Albert   As have I.

Cordelia   You are destined to be a successful writer, Albert, and deservedly so.

Albert   Sweet Cordelia. How can you think I can find success without you beside me? [*Pause*]As my intended?

Cordelia   Oh Albert… That cannot be.

Albert   [*remote*] It seems like a dream does it not? I keep expecting to awaken but I know I shall not.

Cordelia   [*sadly*] It is a dream without end.

Albert   A cruel turn of events has inflicted itself upon us.

Cordelia   We are powerless to prevent it.

Edgar   [*now standing*] I can feel their discomfort, father.

Maxwell   I feel it also. [*Pause*] My heart is indeed heavy for them.

Edgar   Can we not relieve their suffering?

Maxwell   [*shakes his head*] I fear their pain runs too deep. For now, we must allow their feelings to run freely. Only then may we determine a way to console them, and they to find some inner peace.

Albert withdraws a hip flask from the inside pocket of his jacket; he unscrews the top, holds the hip flask up and faces the folly.

Albert   To the folly. Ever constant. Ever reliable. May your enchantment live on forever in the hearts of all those affected by your noble presence.

Albert takes a swig from his hip flask.

Maxwell   [*sombre*] And so it will.

Edgar   Amen.

Cordelia   [*poignantly*] A building without purpose.

Albert   [*replaces the hip flask*] And yet pleasing to the eye.

Cordelia   [*looks to Albert*] Which would be its purpose.

Pause.

Albert   [*smiling*] A more convivial time and place. The world seemed so much clearer than it

does now. Our lives less… *complicated.*

Cordelia   I cannot go against my mother's… and my father's… wishes. [*Determined*] I cannot.

Albert   It is I who should be strong and yet I find nothing but weakness lies within my very

being. I am a most feeble example of a man.

Cordelia   You must not think so. We are both an innocent victim of circumstance.

Albert   An ill turn of fortune.

Cordelia   We must look onwards. We have our whole lives before us.

Maxwell   Dear Cordelia. A practical head on such young shoulders.

Edgar   My sister is showing a brave heart.

Maxwell   Indeed she is. And yet great sadness lives within it.

Albert   [*distant*] It seems such a long road ahead. I'm not sure I have the strength to journey it

alone. It seems uncommonly cruel.

Cordelia   Dear sweet Albert. My heart will always be with you.

Albert   And mine with you.

Cordelia   And yet we are destined to live separate lives.

Albert   Such a foul turn of events to befall us.

Cordelia   The cards have been dealt.

Albert   [*irate*] By the Devil himself.

Cordelia   We must play them as best we can.

Albert   A hand we cannot win.

Cordelia   So it would seem.

Albert   If there was some way out of this… [*Looks to the heavens*] Deliver us from this eternal plight I beseech you.

Cordelia   [*desperate*] Oh, Albert...

Albert and Cordelia are as still as statues.

Maxwell   [*in deep thought*] Perhaps there is?

Edgar   Father?

Maxwell and Edgar walk around the still figures of Albert and Cordelia.

Maxwell   After such an earnest plea from Albert perhaps the folly can find relief from their torment.

Edgar   How so?

Maxwell   Its enchantment works in prodigious ways. It can be a powerful force for good.

Edgar   Indeed it can. But how can it be found?

Maxwell   We can only encourage it and have faith it will find a way. Albert and Cordelia must both enter the folly in order for the enchantment to fulfil its destiny.

Albert and Cordelia are animated once again.

Albert   What is to become of us?

Cordelia   We must journey on.

Albert   But to what end?

Cordelia   To our own. It is the way of life.

Albert   [*looks blankly ahead*] Death would be welcome relief.

Cordelia approaches Albert and touches his cheek with her hand.

Cordelia   Albert… please. It breaks my heart to hear you so.

Albert touches Cordelia's hand affectionately.

Albert   Dearest Cordelia.

Cordelia   Dearest Albert.

Maxwell has a revelation.

Maxwell   [*enthusiastically*] Church bells. We must summon church bells Edgar. Time is upon us. Think… fast...

Edgar   Yes Father.

Maxwell and Edgar both cover their ears and close their eyes in concentration. Distant church bells are heard. Maxwell and Edgar are elated with their efforts.

Maxwell/Edgar   [*quietly in unison*] Hurrah.

Albert   A wedding is in progress. A time of joy for a loving couple. If fate had not played its part… What might have been?

Cordelia   Perhaps if we close our eyes…

Albert and Cordelia hold hands and close their eyes and imagine they are in attendance at their own wedding.

Albert   I, Albert Buckley, take thee, Cordelia Hatherton, to be my wedded Wife, to have and to hold from this day forward.

Cordelia   I, Cordelia Hatherton, take thee, Albert Buckley, to be my wedded Husband, to have and to hold from this day forward.

As they both open their eyes, Albert takes a gold ring from his finger.

Albert   With this ring I thee wed.

Cordelia offers her hand, and Albert places the gold ring upon her finger.

Cordelia   It will remain with me for now and for always.

Albert   In life.

Cordelia   As in death.

Albert and Cordelia embrace each other. The church bells are no longer heard.

Maxwell   They have pledged a union for now and forever.

Edgar   Are they married, father?

Maxwell   [*shakes his head*] Their union lives on in the spiritual world. A part of them will be eternally with the other.

Edgar   A happy circumstance.

Maxwell   Indeed it is. For now...

Albert and Cordelia face each other at arm's length.

Albert   This moment will be with me always.

Cordelia   As with me.

Albert and Cordelia gaze in each other's eyes and lean in close as if to kiss.

Maxwell   [*gently*] That cannot be.

A loud clap of thunder intrudes upon their intention.

Albert   [*looks to the sky*] The Gods have made their displeasure heard.

Cordelia breaks from their embrace and turns away.

Edgar   Would it be wrong for them to indulge their feelings, father?

Maxwell   Alas, I fear it would seal their fate in the physical world. A world that will not accept

their undying love for each other.

Edgar   They would suffer hardship?

Maxwell   [*sombrely*] Indeed they would.

Cordelia   [*tearful*] It is a sign from the heavens. Our fate is sealed.

Albert   [*resigned*] So it would seem.

Cordelia   We are to remain brother and sister.

Albert   And so it must be.

Maxwell   A worthy union.

Edgar   They are reconciled, father.

Maxwell   They must enter the folly to seal their bond as brother and sister. I have a notion…

A strange gust of wind is seen rustling the foliage.

Cordelia   [*looks around her*] I feel there is but one thing left to do.

Cordelia enters the steps of the folly and beckons Albert with her outstretched arm.

Albert   [*looks on wistfully in nostalgic recollection*] I do believe you have lost all reason,

Cordelia.

Cordelia   I believe you are quite correct. But nonetheless do please join me because I suddenly

feel quite extravagantly foolish.

Albert   Then I shall join you but only to appease your feelings of foolish guilt.

Albert walks to Cordelia and takes her hand in his. They walk up the steps to the folly.

Edgar   Fate has played a kind hand in cruel circumstance.

Maxwell   I believe the enchantment of the folly has played its part. Of that I am quite sure.

Albert and Cordelia enter the folly and sit facing each other, still holding hands.

Lights fade.

Interval.

Albert's room. Albert writes at his candlelit desk.

> *After a while Albert replaces the pen to its holder, rises, walks to window, and opens the heavy curtains. Early sunlight encroaches the room with its intensity. Albert briefly shades his eyes, and then turns to audience.*

Albert　　It is only in the cold light of day that one truly sees… A full ten years had passed as if in the blink of an eye. My dear friend Claude was now married to Prudence. Their alliance was a happy one. Prudence aglow with the new life that lived within her. A joyful interlude in a time of great uncertainty. Grace was still adamantly independent of nature, and continued her love of art, with the aid of Claude's benevolence. Her work revered by many. [*Long pause*] My dearest brother Felix had his life cut short during his long naval campaign in Egypt; his noble passing a shock to us all. And yet his spirit lived on in that enchanted area. [*Pause*] And as for me… I found myself drifting on a sea of despair. The death of Cordelia at her own hands too cruel to contemplate…

Lights fade.

ACT FOUR

Soulful music.

The enchanted area. Late summer. Nature continues to make its presence felt upon the folly and its surroundings.

> *Enter Claude, Prudence, and Grace, followed by Felix, from left. Prudence walks arm in arm with Claude; Grace, holding sketch pad and pencil, and Felix, follow closely behind them. They have each aged accordingly, except Felix who retains the same youthfulness and attire as when first seen in the enchanted area of the folly.*

Prudence　　Oh look, Grace. We are returned.

Prudence breaks free from Claude and touches the statue of the angel, as if meeting an old acquaintance.

Grace   It is still so beautiful here.

Claude   Its charm has not diminished through time's passing.

Prudence   Yes. It is still enchanting here, is it not?

Grace   [*looks around her*] Although many years have elapsed I still feel that same sense of awe and wonder from when we were first here.

Felix   It *is* strangely beguiling. It feels quite *unreal* to be present here once more. [*Looks puzzled*] After all this time...

Claude   Much water has passed under the bridge since our last visitation.

Prudence   [*reflective*] Muddied by the passing of loved ones.

Claude   And yet cleansed by our joyful union. [*Looks to Prudence*] Dearest wife.

Claude reaches out his hand to Prudence who accepts it warmly.

Prudence   Dearest husband.

Claude and Prudence gaze at each other in deep affection.

Grace   I declare… How you both do glow. It warms the heart to see it. [*Emotionally*] I am happy for you both.

Felix   [*enthusiastically*] As am I. Wholeheartedly. [*Looks to Grace tenderly*] A good match has been made indeed.

Grace wipes a tear from her eye with her silk handkerchief.

Grace   You must think me a weak fool.

Felix   [*gently*] Your emotion is a beauty to behold.

Prudence   [*to Grace*] Dearest sister. You have been so gracious in the most turbulent of times.

Your support has meant more to us than you will ever know.

Claude   My wife and I thank you most kindly Grace.

Grace   It is I who should give thanks.

Prudence   How can that be?

Grace   Your happy union has brightened the darkest of days. Without it I fear the world would

be forever bleak and cold.

Prudence   As long as you are in the world that cannot be.

Felix   [*passionately*] I most fervently agree.

Grace   [*to Claude and Prudence*] And I am ever grateful to you both for your patronage.

Without it I would not have been accepted by the Royal Academy. My work would

never have been shown were it not for your kindness.

Claude   Think little of it. Your work stands tall on its own. Established artists, such as Henrietta

Ward, have given your work much credit. I hear your destiny is to be a fortuitous one.

You are a rare talent, Grace.

Felix   Hear hear.

Prudence   If father was still with us, he would be fit to burst with pride.

Grace   That thought has sustained me throughout my efforts. [*Pause*] It is odd, but when I am

at my lowest ebb I feel his presence, which strengthens my resolve. [*Looks at her

surroundings*] Even now I feel he is with us still, though I know that cannot be.

Prudence   I too have felt as such. Our sister would scoff at such imaginings, I am sure.

Grace   Poor Cordelia. Sent to Canterbury on such an obvious false errand.

Felix   Sent to Coventry more like. [*Serious*] A cruel but… *understandable*… undertaking.

Claude   And poor Albert. He has immersed himself entirely in writing with the intensity of a mad man. It is as though he were possessed. And yet I know him well. My old friend is grieving for that which he cannot have… He has also taken to the drink with utmost abandon. [*Looks blankly ahead*] I feel his sorrow most deeply.

Felix   [*distant*] As do I. My poor brother.

Claude   [*earnestly*] I fear for him.

Prudence   [*now resolute*] We must not dwell on life's cruel ways. My father would not have wished it. [*Thoughtful pause*] We have some good news to share. [*To Claude*] Do we not, husband?

Claude   [*filled with pride*] Indeed we do.

Grace   Do tell. I am intrigued.

Felix   As am I.

Prudence   We are to hear the patter of tiny feet. [*Beams*] I am with child.

Grace   I am at a loss for words.

Felix   This is indeed a joyous occasion.

Grace   Can you be sure?

Prudence   Quite sure. The doctor has confirmed as such.

Felix   [*elated*] Such happy news.

Grace   I am to be an aunt?

| Claude | Indeed you are. Aunt Grace. |

Maxwell and Edgar enter silently from the rear of the folly. They have a look of concern about them as they survey the scene before them from within the folly.

| Grace | I am so happy for you both. |

Grace embraces Prudence.

| Felix | Yes. Hearty congratulations are in order. This is a most pleasing outcome. |

Maxwell and Edgar walk slowly down the front steps of the folly.

| Prudence | If it is a girl we shall name her after her aunts, Grace and Cordelia. |

| Grace | Such an honour to bestow upon me and upon our eldest sister. |

| Prudence | No more than you both deserve. Dearest sister. |

| Claude | [*brimming with pride*] And if a boy he shall be named Felix Edgar Denning. |

| Felix | [*boyishly*] I am cock-a-hoop. This is a most gracious honour you have granted me and my dear departed brother. My sincerest congratulations to you both. |

Felix offers his hand to Claude who oddly does not take it. Maxwell shakes his head in sadness. Felix looks to Claude in disbelief. Pause.

| Maxwell | [*gently*] They cannot hear you. |

Felix turns to Maxwell and Edgar.

| Felix | [*shocked*] Mister Hatherton... Edgar... What?... Is it really you? This *cannot* be possible... What kind of dark magic is at play? |

Claude takes Grace's hand in both of his in celebration. Claude, Prudence and Grace are now as still as statues as the light slowly fades on them.

Edgar   And your presence cannot be seen by them, brother Felix.

Felix   But you are… You are…

Maxwell   Deceased? Sadly, that is true. [*Pause*] As are you, my boy. As are you. Be brave and be not afraid. It is the way of things.

Felix   [*angrily*] This *cannot* be. I am in a dream and will wake up momentarily. [*Shakes his head and points at Maxwell and Edgar*] You are just a… a… figment of my imagination. [*Desperately*] All of this… [*To himself*] A symptom of temporary insanity perhaps? This madness must end. NOW.

A loud clap of thunder is heard, with sudden brief darkness, from overhead. Felix looks to the sky.

Edgar   You must embrace the truth, Felix.

Maxwell   [*earnestly*] Indeed you must. Your safe passage may depend upon it.

Felix   How CAN I? [*Looks around him*] What demons are at play? How can this be? [*Looks pleadingly to Maxwell*] Am I in hell?

Maxwell   Far from it. You are in… *transition*. A moment in time.

Edgar   A happier place.

Felix   But I cannot contemplate such a dark event. How can I be conversing with the dead? Such a bewildering situation.

Maxwell   Then consider this Felix... where were you before you entered this enchanted area?

Felix thinks long and hard.

Felix   [*shakes his head in frustration*] I cannot recall…

Edgar   You must try. Think dear Felix.

Long pause.

Felix [*resigned*] On board ship.

Edgar And what happened? Think hard.

Felix [*looks blankly ahead*] I was Midshipman on board HMS Temeraire.

Maxwell And what took place?

Felix It was during the bombardment of Alexandria in Egypt. [*Looks to Maxwell and Edgar*] Admiral Seymour ordered us to protect British interests in the Suez Canal at all costs.

Maxwell We are making progress. Pray continue...

Felix [*looks anxiously to Maxwell*] It is something of a blur...

Edgar [*gently*] It is to be expected.

Maxwell Indeed. But let your mind drift back to that fateful time.

Long pause.

Felix We engaged the enemy. [*Felix walks up the steps to the folly and looks out*] A most perilous undertaking. Our gunboats shelled the forts between Ras El Tin and Mex with enormous violence. [*Lights are dimmed. Noises from the battle are heard. Felix raises his voice to be heard above the sound of screamed commands and cannon fire*] They returned fire with utmost ferocity. [*Flashes of light amidst darkness pervade the scene. The folly becomes a ship with Felix looking out*] All hell was unleashed that day. The noise and stench of the shelling permeated the air. Our cannons pounded against coastal defences relentlessly despite powerful return from enemy forces. It was my first engagement as an officer in Her Majesty's Royal Navy. The signal command given by Admiral Seymour aboard HMS Invincible was to continue the attack until the enemy was departed from the face of the earth. We continued the attack with renewed concentration. We slaughtered most of the enemy forces. The forts largely destroyed. Fire raged across coastal defences. Victory was within our grasp. [*Looks to Maxwell and Edgar in earnest*] I remained steadfast in my duty to Queen and country.

Maxwell   We are justly proud of your endeavour.

Edgar   Britain is the greater for it.

Maxwell   [*calmly*] And what of *your* outcome Felix?

Long pause. Felix steps down from the folly.

Felix   We came under concentrated fire from the few remaining guns. [*Pause*] Our ship was struck and set ablaze.

The battle's noise slowly abates; violent sea waves are heard and seen amongst the flames.

Maxwell   You must find strength to continue Felix.

Long pause.

Felix   I found myself in the cold dark sea clinging to driftwood. [*Pause*] The lower half of my body torn asunder. Pain beyond measure. I could see several bodies in the water beside me. All gone. It felt as if I were many hours within that raging swell. Holding on for dear life as best I could. I grew weak until I could hold on no longer. I found myself sinking. Ever deeper and deeper into the murky depths of the sea. I recall looking up and seeing a distant and yet beautiful light. It burned with intensity. [*Looks to Maxwell and Edgar*] I was strangely calm. [*Long pause*] I was finally free from pain and anguish. I no longer felt hatred for the enemy nor fear for myself.

The sounds of the sea slowly fade into an eerie silence. The light and sounds of nature slowly begin to return to the enchanted area once more.

Maxwell   You have travelled a long and eventful journey.

Edgar   You can rest easy.

Felix   It feels as if a great weight has been removed from me. I am at peace. [*Looks to Maxwell and Edgar*] It is a good feeling.

Maxwell   You have accepted your fate with great aplomb.

Felix looks down at his legs and then at his apparel.

Edgar   [*enthusiastically*] Glory be.

Felix   It is strange. I am as I was when I first came here all those years ago. I have not changed from that young man. [*Feels his chin and smiles*] Aboard ship I had a beard.

Maxwell and Edgar smile reassuringly.

Maxwell   [*knowingly*] It is the way of things.

Edgar   A moment in time and a happier place.

The light returns upon Claude, Prudence and Grace.

Maxwell   Tell me Felix… what decided you on a life at sea?

Felix looks with affection to Grace. Claude, Prudence and Grace are animated once again.

Felix   My undying affection for your daughter, sir. [*Pause*] For Grace...

Grace   [*to Claude*] I'm sure Felix would have been proud of such an honour. Edgar also. You're very kind.

Claude   [*enthused*] This is indeed a happy day.

Edgar   Indeed it is.

Maxwell   [*to Felix*] I felt as much. It took great courage on your part. A noble and selfless act to remove yourself from a love that cannot be in the physical world. I believe my daughter's feelings for you still burn brightly despite your demise. I believe that is why you find yourself in this enchanted place. To console her in her time of need.

Felix   There was not a day that went by that I did not think of her.

Maxwell   [*sombrely*] Nor she you. She still grieves your loss.

Felix looks to Maxwell in shocked surprise.

Felix   I did not know...

Edgar   My sister's affection for you is eternal. I am proud to call you brother.

Felix clasps Edgar's shoulder in celebration.

Felix   As I am you.

Maxwell, Edgar and Felix survey the scene before them.

Prudence   [*softly to Grace*] Felix's passing was most unexpected. I know you thought fondly of him.

Grace looks to the folly with nostalgia.

Grace   It is most odd. I feel his presence still, but I know it cannot be.

Felix   Dearest Grace.

Grace opens her sketch pad and looks at her drawing of Felix.

Grace   I will always have his likeness to remind me of a moment in time that was simpler and forever happy for me. [*Pause*] And for him also.

Felix stands before Grace and touches her hands under the sketch pad. Grace looks up from the sketch pad with shocked wonder.

Prudence   Why, Grace, you look as if you have seen a ghost.

Long pause.

Grace   A most bewildering occurrence.

Claude   What ails you?

Grace   [*to herself*] A trick of the light perhaps?

Felix   [*gently*] I did not mean to startle you. Forgive me.

Prudence   What did you see that moved you so?

Grace   The picture…

Maxwell   [*to Felix*] You must be careful of your new-found powers. They can be a most potent force.

Grace   It turned from a mere likeness to flesh and blood. It was as if Felix were there on the page itself. [*Pause*] His eyes were so alive... So… expressive.

Edgar   Praise be.

Grace looks to Claude and Prudence.

Grace   [*to herself*] He is at peace. [*Reflective pause*] He met with such a violent but noble end. [*Pause*] I grew to love him though he may not have known it.

Felix looks to the skies.

Felix   She loved me. [*Looks to Maxwell and Edgar*] She *loved* me. I heard it from her own fair lips. [*Looks to Grace*] Such joy.

Maxwell   I am happy for you.

Edgar   As am I.

Claude   He was a fine young man. To die in such a way… words fail me...

Prudence   [*looks about her*] I have always been of the opinion that this is an enchanted place.

                Now I know it to be true.

Grace   [*to herself*] A part of me will always be here.

Felix   [*smiling wistfully*] I will wait an eternity for you.

Claude   [*gestures to Grace and Prudence*] Come. We must journey back. Time is marching on.

                [*Looks to the sky*] It will soon be dark. Our carriage awaits. We must away.

                Claude and Prudence turn and begin to make their journey home.

Prudence   Perhaps one day we will return to this place and rekindle our memories? For old time's

                sake.

                Grace gives one last look about her before leaving.

Grace   [*ominously*] I am certain of it. [*Pause*] I will return.

                Felix, Maxwell and Edgar witness the ongoing departure of Claude, Prudence and

                Grace.

Maxwell   Journey long and safe. And be assured we will watch over you all.

Edgar   For now and forever.

                Felix fixedly watches Grace's departure.

Felix   [*gently*] Until we meet again. [*Melancholic*] Sweet Grace.

                Exit Claude, Prudence and Grace. Long pause.

Maxwell   [*to Felix*] It is well that you have given Grace some comfort in her hour of need.

Edgar   My sister's heart is full thanks to you, brother Felix.

Felix   My heart is also full. I shall not rest until our paths meet once more in this enchanted

place. May her life be long and happy.

Maxwell   [*serene*] You know, I believe it will.

Felix   [*to Maxwell and Edgar*] Before my untimely end, if you were to ask me what is the most

important part of creation I would have said it is the air that we breathe, but it is *love*

that transcends all before us. If we have *love,* then we have life. Even when life has

fulfilled its destiny, it is *love* that lives on in the hearts and minds of those still living,

and those who have passed into the spirit world before their final rest. It is all powerful

and all consuming. If we have *love* we have no need for fear and hate. [*Pause*] My heart

is full with my eternal *love* for Grace; and for *love* of my fellow man.

Maxwell   The world would be a better place if all in the physical world shared such wisdom. It is

in us all to find love instead of hate. Sadly, it is a lesson in history that has yet to be

learned. Perhaps in time man will come to realise the futility of hate over love.

Perhaps…

Edgar   It may take all the time in the world, father.

Maxwell   [*solemnly*] Then there is hope.

The light within the enchanted area slowly begins to fade leaving pale moonlight.
Rapid flashes of light amidst dark pervade the enchanted area as though night and day
were rapidly interchanging.

Felix   [*surveys the scene before him*] What is upon us?

Maxwell   In the spirit world time can move with great haste. [*Looks to Felix*] It is the way of

things.

The folly is now alive with an eerie glow.

Edgar   Our time draws closer.

Maxwell looks to the folly with concern etched upon his face as he can sense the aura of impending tragedy. A strong gust of wind sweeps through the enchanted area bringing with it the prospect of adversity.

Maxwell   NO. [*Looks to the heavens*] Please. I beg of you.

Lightning and thunder violently show their displeasure.

Edgar   [*alarmed*] The spirit Gods are angry.

Maxwell   [*distraught*] Not *her*... [*Pause*] *Please...*

Edgar   [*distant*] Cordelia...

Felix   [*loudly*] Mister Hatherton? [*Pause*] Edgar?

As the noise abates, a faint mist envelops the enchanted moonlit area. Cordelia is seen slowly entering the folly from the rear steps; she retains the same youthfulness and attire as when first seen in the enchanted area of the folly. Maxwell, Edgar and Felix look on, transfixed by the scene before them.

Cordelia   Do my eyes deceive me? What witchcraft is at work? How am I returned to this place from such an inglorious end?

Edgar   Can Cordelia not see us, father?

Maxwell   [*despondently shakes head*] She is the taker of her own life. Her journey to rest is a solitary one.

Edgar   My poor dear sister.

A dishevelled Albert enters from left. An opened bottle of strong spirits is held in his hand.

Felix   My brother…

Cordelia sees Albert, and slowly walks down the steps of the folly.

Maxwell   A sorry turn of events.

Cordelia   Albert...

Edgar   Can we not intervene, father?

Maxwell   [*shakes head*] I fear not.

Albert   [*slurring*] Why? Oh why? The pain cuts so deep. [*Pause*] You should have *lived*. It is *I* who should have departed kicking and screaming from this sorry world into the next. And yet I persist. What justice is there to be had? And what life do I have? I am a wretch of a man who drinks to forget that which haunts each day and night. [*Drinks the last from his bottle and throws the empty bottle aside*] And so I find myself here in this place of sanctuary as though drawn like a moth to a flame... with the same inevitable conclusion.

Cordelia   Albert... you must be strong. I beg of you.

Albert looks to the folly.

Albert   It is fitting. My life is as redundant as that of a folly. Of no purpose other than to exist for the sake of existence. I cannot contemplate a more worthless proposition. It is no life at all...

Cordelia   Please... Do not speak so...

Albert   How can I live when the one person I loved more than life itself lives no more? It is because of me that she is no longer present in this world. [*Holds out his hands in front of him and examines them*] I cannot in good conscience live out my days with such blood on my hands.

Cordelia   I was the sole cause of my own... *misfortune.* You are without blame.

Albert retrieves a small bottle of poison from his pocket and removes the stopper.

Albert   A potion that will remedy that which has ailed me for so long. [*Looks to the heavens*] May god forgive me.

Cordelia rushes to Albert and faces him; she places her hands upon his. Although he cannot see Cordelia, Albert feels her presence.

Cordelia   Albert… Please do not do *this*. I beg of you. Live.

Albert recoils in shock.

Albert   How can it *be*? I sense her near, and yet I know that she is no longer of this world. Perhaps a trick of the mind? A cruel symptom of my dependency?

Cordelia   It is something more potent than mere earthly affairs.

Albert   How strange I feel.

Cordelia   Embrace it, dearest Albert.

Albert   A calmness has entered me. I know now that I must endeavour.

Maxwell   Praise be.

Albert   It is love. I *feel* it.

A light flickers and grows with intensity at the rear of the folly.

Cordelia   My time is near…

Cordelia removes her ring, and places it in Alberts's hand. Albert looks at the gold ring in wonder.

Albert   A token of our love.

Cordelia   For now and forever...

Albert   Cordelia...

Cordelia   I must away. Farewell… my love.

> *Cordelia enters the folly and departs down the rear steps. The light slowly fades. Albert empties the contents of the small bottle to the ground, and exits stage left. Maxwell, Edgar and Felix embrace each other as they watch Albert's departure.*

Lights fade.

Albert's room. Albert continues to write at his candlelit desk. A gold ring is before him on the desk.
> *He stops writing, replaces the pen to its holder, and picks up the ring, and examines it in the light from the candle.*

Albert   A ring of truth… [*Long pause. Albert puts the ring on his finger, fills his glass from the decanter and takes a long drink; he rises, drink in hand, and walks to the portrait of Cordelia that hangs upon the wall, and gazes at it.*] By the kind hand of Grace. Likeness beyond measure… [*Glances at the ring on his finger*] Keepsakes that will be with me until my own time is come... [*Turns to audience*] Innumerable years passed like thieves in the night. Lives lost and found, as is the way of existence. The spirits lived on in that enchanted place, and found themselves nearing the closing of their own intended passage…

Lights fade.

ACT FIVE

Soulful music.

The enchanted area. Winter. A sprinkling of snow is seen upon the dilapidated folly and surrounding area. A thin mist envelopes the cold setting, as faint daylight casts its dying embers of otherworldly glow.

139

Edgar and Felix stand adjacently on the edge of the folly, between pillars, looking out. Maxwell stands before the folly looking to the sky. A distant church bell sounds a regular slow deathly toll, as though a manifestation of that which is to come...

Maxwell   [*philosophical*] The air hangs heavy with expectancy. Our intended passage is near. We have ventured a long way from times past. [*Quizzical look*] I sense a sea of change is upon us. It is a new world. An un*certain* world. A new order. [*Pause*] I believe the hands of time have brought us closer to our intended destiny. [*Looks to Edgar and Felix in earnest*] Whatever may present itself we must embrace it with arms open and hearts wide. [*Long pause*] Our moment in time approaches. [*Pause*] I *sense* it.

Felix   I am ready to confront that which is before us and to welcome the consequence. We have travelled far to this point in time. [*Looks to Edgar*] There is no turning back from this moment hence…

Edgar   [*blankly*] No turning back…

Pause.

Maxwell   Our path has been long...

Edgar   And now we are at a crossroad…

Maxwell   [*sombre*] Yes. [*Pause*] It is one we *all* must face. [*Pause*] In the end…

Long pause.

Felix   I am proud to stand with you both in our ultimate journey.

Edgar   As am I. I know our destiny is at hand. I too can sense it and I am happy to face what will come. [*Sincerely*] I am at peace with the world and all within it. My life has been made full despite its early end, and for that I give thanks. [*Looks to Maxwell*] It is a blessing.

Maxwell   It is well said for one so eternally young. I will be forever proud of you and your spirit Edgar, as I am of you and yours Felix.

Felix steps down from the folly and looks about him.

Felix   The world has changed. [*Looks to Maxwell and Edgar*] We are spirits from the past now present in the future. How strange it *feels*. It is much to absorb and yet I know from somewhere deep within me that all will be well.

Edgar   It is indeed a world I am not familiar with. [*Looks to the sky*] I have witnessed curious sights. [*Looks to Maxwell*] Machines that roam the sky, father. A strange but magnificent vision. Such clever invention…

Maxwell   I have seen them also Edgar. They *are* a wonder to behold. The very *essence* of invention. They have delivered people to far off lands. A wondrous feat of endeavour as with all new machinery. [*Thoughtful pause*] And yet they have also delivered great destruction. [*Long pause*] It seems the advent of time has not tempered man's insatiable appetite for war.

As darkness begins to descend, a faint rumble of thunder is heard followed by intermittent flashes of lightning. A sudden gust of wind enters the enchanted area, making the foliage shudder violently.

Felix   [*looking upwards*] Our time approaches. It is a sign... of that which is to come. [*Looks to Maxwell and Edgar*] Perhaps the final piece of the jigsaw...

Maxwell   Yes. Our time is upon us. [*Looks to Edgar and Felix*] Be not afraid of what may betide us.

Edgar   [*calmly*] It is most strange... I am not afraid... I welcome it willingly.

Felix   [*seriously*] As do I.

An old woman dressed in black, who walks with the aid of a walking stick, enters left. She carries a black leather bag, and is in obvious distress. She stands and looks about her in bewilderment, oblivious to Maxwell, Edgar and Felix.

Maxwell [*whispers*] Can it be?

Maxwell, Edgar and Felix observe the old woman's entrance with intrigue. Long pause. The wind subsides to a gentle breeze.

Grace [*frightened*] What has become of me? [*Stands and looks about her in puzzlement. Long pause*] How do I find myself within this place? Is it just another dark dream? [*Pause*] A mad illusion brought on by infirmity of the mind perhaps? [*Gravely*] I have known many of late... haunting visions and voices that enter my very soul unannounced and plague me still. They are the death of me. Of that I am sure...

Felix approaches Grace. Edgar looks on from the folly.

Felix [*gently*] She is so frail.

Grace looks through Felix and sees the folly before her.

Grace [*now calmed*] So long ago... It has been a lifetime and yet I feel the same sense of awe as when I was but a child. [*Pause*] This was and will always be a place of enchantment. I am sure of it.

Maxwell Such perception. It is something that never strays.

Edgar steps down from the folly and faces Grace.

Edgar Dearest sister. You have enjoyed a long life. I am glad.

Grace I forget so much of late and yet my mind is filled with recollections of times past long ago. Ghosts from my early life that live within me still. They have haunted me for many a year. I have longed to return to this place… but it is only now that I know the time to be right to do so.

Grace shivers from the cold.

Maxwell   [*to himself*] It is as I thought.

Grace   My aged blood is not what it once was. It cannot sustain me as it once did. My time is near...

Felix   [*concerned*] You are cold.

Felix wraps his arms momentarily around Grace's shoulders.

Grace   [*no longer shivering*] How strange…

Edgar   Is she not well Father?

Maxwell shakes his head despondently.

Maxwell   I fear not. Her spirit is strong… but her flesh… and her mind… the physical world can be an unmerciful place.

Felix   [*triumphant*] She has returned. As she said she would. [*Turns to Maxwell and Edgar*] It is a miracle of nature. After such a time...

Maxwell   A miracle indeed. Her inner spirit has delivered her. It is a potent force unlike any other.

Grace stands, transfixed, as if in another time and place.

Grace   [*looks into the distance*] Who are *they* to judge *me*? They think me of weak mind. As though my words are that of a mad person. [*Exultant*] My work has been seen by the King himself. I am a woman of standing. I have risen above those who would see me chained to servitude. I am and always will be of independent nature.

| **Felix** | She has retained that which defined her in her youth despite her advanced years and malaise. |

| **Maxwell** | [*melancholic*] My dearest Grace. I know you cannot hear or see us but be aware that our love for you remains undimmed despite the passing of so many a year. You are and will always be daughter of mine. Feel *safe* now in the knowledge that you are amongst those who will always love you. |

Grace stands still and looks around her, as though struck by an epiphany. Long pause.

| **Grace** | [*smiling*] How oddly at peace I feel. [*Pause*] It is as though a light has been cast upon the shadow that I felt within me. It has lifted my soul. [*Long pause*] This is still an enchanted place. |

| **Edgar** | My sister is touched by the power of your words. |

| **Felix** | She is delivered by the power of *feeling*. |

| **Maxwell** | I believe it to be so. It is sad that so very few of the living have such facility. |

| **Edgar** | Perhaps it is why her art is so… accomplished? |

| **Maxwell** | I believe it is within all people of creative ability. As well as all those that care beyond material things. |

Grace looks to the folly.

| **Grace** | [*transfixed*] The folly... [*Long pause*] It has long been sadly neglected and yet I can sense that it retains the same dignity it once possessed. It has aged as do we all. I must sit within it and gather my thoughts... |

Grace slowly proceeds to walk up the steps to the folly.

| **Felix** | She is seeking the enchantment of the folly. |

Maxwell   It is her destiny.

Grace sits down within the folly, her weight pressed upon her walking stick before her, and looks blankly out in contemplation.

Edgar   Is Grace thinking of the past?

Maxwell   If you listen intently you will hear for yourself.

Edgar and Felix stand before the folly, enraptured.

Grace   [*ponders*] But where to begin? [*Pause*] Ah yes… My beloved brother… I still think of him… Even now…

Echoed voices that resonate from the past within the enchanted area occasionally fill the air.

Edgar   *Must you draw everything that you see?…*

Edgar   [*in awe*] I hear it, father. My own voice.

Grace   *Of course. How else will we remember where we've been and what we've seen when we're old and grey? It is a moment in time that will last forever…*

Edgar   *A moment in time… You are funny Grace. I intend never to be old and grey. I shall stay forever young…*

Felix   Such words... It is as if you foretold your own destiny.

Edgar   [*gravely*] I remember it well. As though it was recently said. We had such youthful spirit… Such expectations…

Felix puts his arm briefly upon Edgar's shoulder to comfort him.

Felix   [*brotherly*] It is something that will be with you forever.

Maxwell   Felix is right, my boy. Your spirit soars as high as an eagle in the sky. Be not

despondent.

Edgar   [*sadly*] It is not for me that I feel as I do, but for my sister… [*Looks to Grace*] Time has

left her so frail.

Felix   Her life has been long. [*Long pause*] You are a good and devoted brother.

Maxwell   Her thoughts have touched you as they have me.

Edgar   They were so… clear.

Maxwell   People in the twilight years of their lives have the ability to remember their early days

with great clarity. It remains one of the profound mysteries in the living world.

Felix   It is pleasing to recollect Grace's youthful voice.

Maxwell   [slightly breathless] We must have walked several miles. I must say we deserve a

reprieve. Such splendid isolation…

Constance   Are you alright my dear? You look tired. Perhaps we should venture back?…

Grace   I remember so vividly. My beloved parents. How I have missed them.

Maxwell   [*sadly*] Constance…

Edgar   Mother…

Pause.

Maxwell   [*shakes head*] Love never leaves…

Prudence   Perhaps you were here in your dreams?…

Cordelia   That sounds rather fanciful? Even for you Prudence. It is a physical impossibility to

inhabit one's dreams…

Felix   A profound statement.

Edgar   My sisters…

Grace   Dear Prudence and Cordelia. [*Long pause*] Both no more...

Felix   Father...

Long pause.

Felix   He was a good upstanding man. A noble man. I hope he knew how much I loved and

respected him.

Maxwell   I am certain of it Felix. He was as proud of you as he was Albert. Of this, I am sure.

Felix smiles in contentment.

Felix	Then I am fulfilled.

Edgar	Such a happy time for all…

Felix	It is why we are returned.

Maxwell	Our moment in time...

Claude *I intend to join the banking profession when I leave. If it will have me. Although I'm not terribly good at mathematics. Unlike Albert who is a natural at everything. Especially sports. I'm Harry Hopeless compared to Albert...*

Grace [*distraught*] Memories are all that linger now. They are all that are left...

Maxwell [*gently*] Memories will never die. They are immortal.

Cordelia *And what of your aspirations Albert? What do you hope to achieve in life?...*

Albert *[slightly embarrassed] You will think me a light hearted fool...*

Cordelia *[serious] I would never think that of you I assure you. Ever...*

Albert *I have pretensions to be a writer. Of plays. For the theatre. [Relieved] There. I have said it...*

Cordelia *But I think that is a wonderful ambition...*

Long pause.

Grace Such tragedy to engulf both of their lives. Love unfulfilled through merciless separation. [*Pause*] But Albert's work lives on. Lives encapsulated on stage for all to see. It is love's sweet revenge...

Felix I am so proud of my elder brother. His work prevails in words and deeds for all to see and hear.

Edgar Has Grace returned to recount memories from her past, father?

Maxwell has a look of serious intent.

Maxwell   [*subdued*] I fear not.

Pause.

Felix   [*gently*] She has come here to die.

Reflective pause.

Maxwell   [*nods head*] It is fate's will.

Grace   Felix…

Felix   *[flamboyantly] Grace… will you do me the very great honour of joining me?..*

Grace   *Oh yes. [A cough from her father. Grace turns to him] With your permission of course father?..*

Maxwell   *[warmly] Granted my dearest young Grace...*

Grace   [*animatedly*] I felt so alive with love and yet I was so childishly young and inexperienced in such things; but it is a feeling I have carried with me throughout my long years. [*Pause*] It has never left me.

Felix stands at the steps of the folly before Grace.

Felix   [*gravely*] It is a feeling I know well...

Grace rises in fright, as if she has seen a ghost.

Grace   [*alarmed*] I feel his presence but I know it cannot be so.

Felix backs off, slightly in fear.

Felix   Forgive me Grace... I did not mean to startle you.

Grace   [*boldly*] Is this what it means to be mad? [*Pause*] To feel the presence of the dead as though they are still here among the living; [*long pause*] to dwell forever in days long since passed; to see faces from years gone by as though they exist still in the present; [*looks about her*] to hear voices that fill the air with words as clear as though they were just uttered, but were said when I was but a child. It is as though the dead still had breath in their broken bodies when I know they have not. [*Pause*] They visit me at night while I sleep, and I receive them willingly in my dreams. [*Walks slowly down the steps of the folly with her sketch pad clutched to her breast*] Is it madness to recollect those who lay long-buried beneath the cold wet soil as if they still walk above it? [*Stands before the folly, looking out*] My mind is so full with such illusion that I no longer have the capacity to know what is now… [*with pathos*] and what was *then*. [*Pause*] I have lived a long existence. I have seen much death and visited many headstones whose words have long since faded into obscurity. This mad obsession with death is not of my making. [*Emotionally*] It is nature's way of securing the memory of those dearest to me who are now forever lost to this world. [*Looks briefly at the statue*] They come to me as if by angels… and live again. [*Long pause*] And now it is *I* who can feel the cold wind of death against my face. [*Touches her cheek gently*] Who is there to grieve for *me* when *I* am lost to this world? [W*alks to centre of enchanted area and places the sketch pad on the ground; she gently kneels beside it*] If there is a greater power in this existence, as I believe there to be, receive me unto you I beseech you. [*Looks to the heavens as if in prayer; scattered lightning is briefly seen*] My body craves the everlasting solace and peace that death brings; [*defeatedly*] it has not the energy nor the will to fight against it as it once did. [*Long pause*] I am… ready… to sleep.

Grace lays down upon the ground, her head now resting upon the sketch pad; her eyes close and she sleeps peacefully. The light slowly fades on Grace, as death envelops her frail body, and she finally breathes no more. A light flickers at the rear of the folly and becomes brighter until it rages incessantly with intensity. A figure from the light emerges from the rear steps of the folly; Grace has returned as she once was when she first entered the enchanted area.

Felix   Grace…

Grace stands in the middle of the folly and looks around her in bewilderment. Edgar and Maxwell look to Grace in silent awe.

Grace   [*distant*] I am returned.

Maxwell   [*with great import*] Our moment in time is now. We must enter the light.

Edgar   Let us depart together as one.

Grace holds out her arm beckoning Felix, Edgar, and Maxwell to join her. Felix enters the folly and holds Grace's hand, and they embrace. Maxwell puts a fatherly arm around Edgar's shoulders and they too enter the folly. They all walk down the rear steps of the folly and are seen no more. The light at the rear of the folly slowly flickers and fades until it dies as peacefully as Grace, Felix, Edgar, and Maxwell.

Lights fade.

EPILOGUE

Albert's room. Albert puts down his pen and leans back in his seat, in quiet contemplation.

After a long period of reflection Albert solemnly drinks the remaining spirits from his glass and instinctively picks up the decanter to refresh it, but the decanter is now conspicuously empty. Having replaced the empty glass and decanter upon the desk he stares directly ahead as if in a trance.

Albert   It is concluded. This tale's journey has now reached its inevitable destination; a conclusion that is as sure as that which exists within all life; as certain as are the changing seasons of the year. [*Reflective*] We are all destined to make that same fateful arrival... in time. [*Pause*] There may be those who would question the moral of this tale... I do not seek to provide a moralist view. I can only offer that it is from my own thoughts and interpretation, rendered entirely in the spirit of its time and nature, and hope that it be accepted for what it is. For is it not the *spirit* within all of us that yearns to be free? Can we truly say with hearts and minds open that when love is denied its true passage, our lives could ever be the same as they once were? [*Pause*] My life and the lives of countless others throughout this mad and glorious existence remain irreparably tainted by the anguish of just such a dilemma. [*Pause*] I have not sought to make judgement on the nature of love's path but to reflect my own experience through words that now seem unworthy in their execution. I am merely a conveyor of my own sentiments and expression. [*Pause*] What is the *meaning* of this life... as with love... but to live it with every breath at your disposal while you are able? It is a conundrum as haunting and unknowing as that of a folly. [*Long pause*] The play has ended but the drama lives on... for are we not *all* players in our own moment in time?

Albert extinguishes the candle.

Lights fade.

153

Play ends.

Visitors from a Lost World

A two act play

Written by Colin Fantham

<u>CHARACTERS</u>

Arthur (elderly)

Arthur (young)

Joey

Dotty

Mildred

Eddie

Gerald

Hilda

Felix

Bill

Doctor

Nurse

Soulful music

PROLOGUE

Spring 2019. Centre stage. A dilapidated small dark flat, once occupied by Arthur, now desolate, and infested with cobwebs and grime, situated in a tower block building somewhere in London. Shabby Christmas decorations festoon the walls. In the middle of this dire setting is a broad window through which can just be seen other buildings far in the distance below, which accentuates the height and isolation of the location. Right of centre a tall bookcase upon which are an assortment of books, papers and framed photographs beside which is a record player on a stand with an abundance of old LPs piled up underneath; left of centre an armchair and a brass standard lamp; far left, set away from the wall, is a small dining table and two chairs; upon the table are: a fish bowl containing a small amount of murky green water, a small container of fish food, an old radio, and an empty whisky glass beside an empty bottle of whisky.

> *Felix, dressed in full protective plastic clothing, stands left of centre stage busily engaged in tying up several large bags of clearance debris amassed from the other rooms. Felix is an experienced old hand at clearances of this nature. Bill, who is also dressed in full protective clothing, enters from stage right dragging a full bag behind him; he is much younger and more inexperienced than Felix. Bill pulls down his hood and face mask and joins Felix in the task of tying up each bag.*

Bill   Full of flies in that kitchen. I'll be glad when this job's done, Felix. Makes you feel sick. [*Long pause*] And the *smells…*

> *Bill takes out cigarette roller and pouch of tobacco. Felix lowers his hood and face mask.*

Felix   This is only your first clearance. You'll get used to it. When you've been doing this for as long as I have. Imagine how the forensics feel? They have to view the bodies.

Determine cause of death. Not a pretty sight. Or smell… We've cleared the worst

bits of the property. Only a couple of rooms to go.

Bill   It's alright for you. You're riding off into the sunset.

Bill proceeds to make a rolled-up cigarette.

Felix   [*nods*] My last job. [*Pause*] I'm going to miss this line of work.

Bill looks to Felix in bewilderment. Long pause.

Bill   Are you mad? How can anyone miss *this* line of work? It has to be the worst job in

the *world*.

Felix   It's the satisfaction you get when you've *finished* the job. I look back on each

completed clearance with a sense of achievement.

Bill   I'm not sure I can work for as long as you have doing this. It's a wonder you can

sleep at night. This is hell on earth.

Felix   I was like you when I first started. It's a shock to all the senses. But then you come

to terms with it.

Bill   How?

Felix   You have to think of the client. It's a service. After all, it's not going to clean itself. I

see it as a duty. A duty to the deceased. They were once flesh and blood, just like

you and me. [*Pause*] When you think of it, we're quite… privileged.

Bill   Privileged?

Felix   This was where the client drew his last breath. [*Pause*] Gives me goosebumps when I

think about that.

Bill   You're a cheerful old sod, aren't you?

Felix	It's part of life's journey, Bill. Death. Happens to all of us. Eventually.

Bill	How old was he?

Felix	I'm told he had a good innings.

Bill	When I go, I'll have people around me. Friends, family. I won't end up like… *this*.

Felix smiles to himself.

Felix	Everybody thinks that. You can't predict the future. Hopefully there'll be somebody there who gives a toss. But there's no guarantees in life… or in death.

Bill shakes his shoulders as though suddenly cold.

Bill	Gives me the willies.

Felix	[*shrugs nonchalantly*] Nature of the beast.

Bill	Nothing surprises you anymore does it?

Felix looks on in solemn contemplation.

Felix	I've seen just about everything you can imagine in this line of work. Rats. Insects. Blood. Excrement all *over* the place. It's never pretty. You get accustomed to it. Human nature being what it is.

Bill	I'm not sure I'll ever get used to it. How do people end *up* like this?

Felix	They die. Alone. No visitors to look in on them. The place falls to the elements. As do *they*. Happens a lot. More than you think. [*Pause*] Not their fault. That's life, I suppose. I feel sorry for them. It's sad that they should die on their own. It's not fair, is it? Nobody should be that… isolated. You hope it never happens to you. But you never know. Life can be very harsh sometimes.

Bill	It's insane.

Felix   The tragic thing is that… once we've swept everything up… cleaned… fumigated… the property gets sold on and it will be like the poor soul never even existed. Like he never even *had* a life. Everything he had, all his memories, was wrapped up in this place and soon it will be… gone. [*Looks around him*] If these walls could talk… I get the same feeling every time I do a death clearance. It's like an aura… I can almost feel a presence… Like we're being watched over…

Lights fade.

ACT ONE

Christmas 2018. Arthur's flat, elevated stage left. It is neat and tidy with brightly coloured Christmas decorations. Upon the table is a fish bowl full of clear water with a goldfish busily swimming around it. Beside the fish bowl is a small tube of fish food, an old radio, a glass of whisky and recently opened bottle of whisky. It is late in the evening.

Arthur sits at the armchair reading an old book. Arthur is an elderly distinguished looking man with a head of silver hair; he wears a white shirt, blue cravat, long dark cardigan, grey slacks, beige socks and comfortable slippers. A pair of reading glasses, attached to a thin chain, are perched triumphantly on the end of his nose. The light from the standard lamp projects a pale light upon him and his surroundings. After a period of time he closes the book with some satisfaction, removes his glasses, and rises from his seat. He places the book down on the armchair and looks in at his aquatic companion. He picks up the fish food container and sprinkles a tiny amount of fish food into the bowl.

Arthur Well, Merlin, that's another book read. I must say you can't beat a gruesome murder mystery. It rounds the day off nicely, doesn't it? There's something oddly reassuring when you read about other people's dark frailties, don't you think? Makes you feel warm inside… and slightly smug, of course. [*Replaces the fish food container*] That means I shall be off to the library again tomorrow. A chance to communicate with another member of the human race other than myself… company accepted. I must have read all the crime novels at that library twice over. [*Sentimental pause*] It's always nice to meet other people when the opportunity presents itself. When I do the weekly shop they always ask me how I am. Of course, when there's a queue a mile long behind you there isn't much time for a proper chinwag. [*Picks up his glass from the table and holds it lovingly*] We've spent many a year in this flat, haven't we

Merlin? Had some interesting chit chats along the way. I have to say you're a *very* good listener. We get on pretty well, don't we? Of course, there was that time I accidentally left the pepper pot by your bowl. [*Shakes his head and tuts*] A very unfortunate incident that was. [*Pause*] You swam round that little bowl so fast it was like a spin *dryer* going off. [*Incidentally*] Half the water had *evaporated* by the time you'd calmed down. But you've never held a grudge. Never complained. I've been very lucky to have a flatmate as easy going as you. Of course, we've had our difference of opinion over Brexit, but all in all we've always remained on good terms. [*Long Pause*] I've been thinking a *lot* about the past lately. It's funny, when you get older, and nearer to the Grim Reaper, your mind drifts back to when you were young. You suddenly remember names and faces from *years* ago. The irony is I can't remember what I had for breakfast, but I can remember people from fifty years ago like it was yesterday. I can even remember my old classmates from when I was knee high. And the teachers too. They used to whack you with a stick back then if you misbehaved – which I did, of course. Hurt like hell. Some of them were a bit too keen on it for my liking. I swear to God some of them took great *pleasure* in it. I suppose they took it out on us when they were having a bad day. [*Long pause*] There seemed to be a lot of those back then… [*Pause*] Did I ever tell you of the time I met Dotty? Stop me if I've already told you. I was in National Service in those days. 1955. Over sixty years ago… Woolwich it was. I was put in an army uniform that itched like hell, and told I was a soldier. We were paid less than two quid a week… I lost most of that playing pontoon. [*Pause*] We didn't have a clue about being in the army. Two weeks basic training and then eight weeks of Corps training. And then the passing out parade. By that time you were so knackered you *felt* like passing out. But it was a proud moment for me and especially for my dear old mum, may she rest in peace. [*Stands up straight and briefly salutes Merlin with great vigour*] Private Arthur Peaty reporting for duty sir. I was on leave while we were waiting to be shipped out to Germany. That's when I met her – Dotty I mean. Me and my mate Joey had just missed the bus...

It was late at night and we had to get back to barracks, otherwise we'd be up for spud bashing the next day…

Arthur sits at the dining table looking out in deep thought.

Lights fade on the flat. It is 1955. We see, downstage centre left, a bus stop by the side of a road. The lights of various restaurants, pubs and houses can be seen at the rear of the stage. The loud roar of an old bus is heard fading into the distance; we also hear the sounds of street life in the background.

Young Arthur and his friend Joey enter hurriedly from stage right. They are dressed in full army uniforms of that time. Arthur runs past the bus stop looking into the distance. Joey stops just before the bus stop.

Joey   [*breathlessly*] Bollocks.

Arthur   [*hands on hips getting his breath back*] I *knew* we shouldn't have had that last pint. I *told* you but you wouldn't listen.

Joey   [*hurt*] Nobody forced you to drink it.

Arthur   We'll be on a charge for sure. The next bus is *hours* away.

Joey   Maybe if you drank a little quicker instead of like a little girl-

Arthur   Oh piss off Joey. I could drink *you* under the table any day.

Joey   A likely story.

          Pause.

Arthur   [*looks at his watch*] I suppose we could walk it...

Joey   [*aghast*] Our barracks are *miles* away, man.

Arthur   [*looks to Joey in disbelief*] We've done twenty mile hikes with full *kit* before now.

Joey   Not after eight pints of bitter we haven't mate. Sod that. [*Dismissively*] You go ahead

if you want, Arthur.

Arthur   No. [*Looks dramatically to where the bus drove off*] A good soldier doesn't leave his

comrades behind.

Joey   What's your name, John Wayne? It's a bus, not a stage coach. This isn't the Rio

Grande. It's Lewisham. We're conscripts remember? The lowest of the low. The real

army hates us.

Arthur   I know. [*Pause*] I swear that's why that Sergeant shouts at us so much.

Joey   He'll give himself a heart attack if he's not careful that one.

Arthur   Fingers crossed. He won't be missed. [*Pause*] Wanker. He's never liked me.

Joey   [*exuberantly*] He's never liked *any*one. I'm told that when he was *born* he slapped the

midwife.

Arthur   Wouldn't surprise me. [*Incidentally*] Probably gave her a good seeing to as well.

Joey looks in bewilderment at Arthur. Long pause.

Joey   [*defeatedly*] Then he's had more luck than we have.

Arthur   Patience is a virtue Joey.

Joey   I'd dance with the *devil* if it meant I could get my rocks off. Bollocks to virtues.

Arthur   Careful what you wish for.

Joey   I just want to spend time with somebody soft and feminine that doesn't have size twelve

feet. Or smell like a navvy's jockstrap. It's not too much to ask, is it?

Arthur   And they say romance is dead. [*Thoughtful*] Would make a nice change though.

Joey   Too patient by far you are. Too… picky. We had a chance with those two earlier but oh, no. Not good enough for Arthur bloody Peaty. They slipped out of our hands like… slippery eels.

Arthur   [*dismissively*] One of them had a five o'clock shadow. The other was old enough to be your old gran.

Joey   [*blankly*] Even so…

Arthur   When I meet somebody who's right for me, I'll know. That's what my mum has always said. "When you meet that special person, your heart will skip a beat and you'll just know." And I believe it too…

Joey   So she's still blissfully married then?

Arthur   [*shakes head despondently*] Divorced. He left home when I was eight. Never came back.

Joey   [*looks up in despair*] Christ.

Dotty and Mildred enter hurriedly from stage right. They are in their early twenties, tipsy, attractive, dressed in bright full circle skirts and smart blouses of the period with contemporary accessories. Arthur and Joey view the new arrivals with salacious interest.

Mildred   [*hurriedly taking off shoes*] My feet are killing me. [*Waves the shoes at Dotty*] These are meant for dancing not doing a hundred-yard dash.

Dotty   Stop moaning Mildred. We'd have got here quicker if we didn't have to stop every minute because of your swollen feet. Why do you always buy shoes that are too small for you anyway?

Mildred   Because they're pretty that's why. Besides, they didn't have them in my size. We can't *all* fit that glass slipper you know.

Joey and Arthur laugh.

Joey   [*to Mildred*] That makes you the ugly sister.

Mildred   [*cuttingly*] I don't remember asking *your* opinion.

Joey looks hurt. Arthur puts his hand on Joey's shoulder in a fake conciliatory gesture.

Arthur   You'll have to excuse my friend Joey. He's not used to talking to members of the opposite sex.

Joey   That's rich. You're not exactly Casanova yourself.

Dotty   [*to Arthur*] Is that right? Bit light in the romantic stakes then?

Arthur   I've never had any complaints. [*Long pause*] What's your name then?

Dotty   Dorothy. My friends call me Dotty. [*Incidentally*] You?

Arthur   Arthur. My friends call me… Arthur.

Dotty and Arthur gaze into each other's eyes.

Dotty   I feel like I know you. Have we met before?

Arthur   [*gently*] Shouldn't that be *my* line?

Mildred   [*to Dotty*] Don't forget we're on early shifts tomorrow. Matron will throw a fit if we're late.

Joey   You're nurses?

Mildred   [*to Arthur*] Sharp as a knife your mate isn't he?

Joey   [*innocently*] It's just that I've never seen nurses as pretty as you.

Mildred   [*dismissively*] I bet you say that to all the nurses.

Joey	[*matter of factly*] No.

| **Mildred** | [*shocked*] Oh… [*Pats hair instinctively*] Thanks. |

| **Dotty** | [*to Arthur*] How long you been in the army then? |

| **Arthur** | Couple of months. We're shipping off to Germany in a few days. |

| **Joey** | National bloody Service. They've got us by the short and curlies. |

| **Mildred** | Not too keen then? |

| **Joey** | We've got no choice. |

| **Arthur** | [*optimistically*] I suppose at least it gets us out of old blighty. See the world a bit. Broaden our horizons as they say. |

| **Dotty** | How long's it for then? |

| **Joey** | [*despondently*] A lifetime… |

| **Arthur** | Two years. |

| **Dotty** | [*absently*] Two years… |

| **Mildred** | My brother's in Germany. Says he loves it. Reckons he may stay on. I suppose it's not for everyone though. |

| **Arthur** | Bit like your line of work. Not everyone's cup of tea. |

| **Dotty** | What… are you saying that emptying bedpans and mopping up vomit isn't universally appealing? |

| **Arthur** | I thought nursing was all about saving people's lives? |

| **Mildred** | That's for the senior nurses. The sisters. We're cadet nurses. |

| **Dotty** | Skivvies. Bottom of the heap. |

Joey   We know how *that* feels…

Arthur   It seems we have a lot in common.

Mildred   At least we don't have to live at home anymore.

Joey   You don't live at home? You've got your own place? No Mum and Dad telling you what time to come home or who you can go out with?

Dotty   Nurse's accommodation just outside the hospital. Me and Mildred are flatmates.

Joey   Flatmates?

Mildred   [*looks to Arthur*] Is he a parrot?

Arthur   [*smiling*] He works in mysterious ways does our Joey.

Joey   I meant you share a room? [*Lusty pause*] Sounds cosy.

Dotty   Well… we share a dining room… and a kitchen.

Mildred   And a bathroom.

Dotty   We have separate bedrooms obviously.

Joey   [*disappointed*] Oh…

Mildred   [*lasciviously to Joey*] Oh. [*Approaches Joey*] Burst your bubble, did it? Think we were lesbians?

Joey   [*unconvincingly*] Of course not. [*Pause*] You're not, are you?

Dotty   [*emphatically*] No. She's not my type. Snores like a pig.

Mildred   [*playfully*] Oi you.

Dotty   [*looks to Arthur*] I prefer the strong silent type myself.

Arthur	[*straightens up*] Do you?
Mildred	Like Gary Cooper in High Noon. [*Dreamy*] He's such a dreamboat. [*Now in a faraway place*] He could have his wicked way with me any day of the week.

Mildred is lost in her imaginings. Joey tries to seize the moment.

Joey	[*hesitantly*] Do… err… do *I* remind you of Gary Cooper?

Mildred looks Joey up and down.

Mildred	No. [*Pause*] More like Charlie Chaplin.

Arthur and Dotty laugh.

Joey	[*hurt*] Well that's friendly I must say.
Mildred	[*placatingly*] I'm joking of course. So sensitive for a soldier.
Joey	I have feelings you know. Beneath this rough manly exterior there *is* a beating heart.
Arthur	That's true. He cried his eyes out when Bambi's mum got shot. [*To Joey*] Didn't you?
Joey	Piss off. I had something in my eye.
Mildred	I think it's sweet.
Joey	[*hopeful*] Do you? [*Fake*] It *was* sad, wasn't it?
Mildred	I like a man who isn't afraid to show his emotions. Like James Stewart in It's A Wonderful Life.
Arthur	The only time *I* cried was when Arsenal lost against Newcastle in the FA cup final. It cut short my dream to be a professional footballer after all that trauma.
Dotty	I think you'd have made a good footballer. [*Looks Arthur up and down*] You've certainly got the physique for it.

Arthur   [*nonchalantly*] Thanks.

Mildred   Is there any money in football?

Joey   [*animatedly*] *Is* there? [*Pause*] I wouldn't mind thirty quid a week just for kicking a

ball around. Spoiled rotten if you ask me...

Arthur   Money isn't everything, Joey.

Joey   Even so... [*absently*] Thirty quid a week…

Dotty   So what happens once you've finished your two years then?

Arthur   How do you mean?

Dotty   What will you do?

Arthur   Get a regular job I suppose. I certainly won't stay in the army.

Joey   Me neither.

Arthur   No. It's not for me. Perhaps train as a car mechanic?

Dotty   [*sensuously*] Oh… Good with your hands then are you?

Arthur   Well… I've changed a gasket or two in my time if that's what you mean...

Dotty   [*disappointedly*] Not really… No…

Mildred   [*to Joey*] And how about you?

Joey   [*thinking hard*] Well… my dad was a plumber as was his dad and his dad before him.

Mildred   You'll be a plumber then?

Joey   Oh, God no…

Mildred   [*to Arthur*] Is there something wrong with him?

Arthur   You'll have to forgive Joey. He was dropped on his head by the midwife. [*Pause*]

Tragic really.

Joey   I was *going* to say that I'd like to run a shop that sells everything to *do* with plumbing.

You know… taps, pipes, tools. That sort of thing.

Mildred   [*contrite*] Be your own boss?

Joey   Well, yes... I suppose so.

Mildred   Ambitious. I like that in a man. It's like Kirk Douglas in Ace In The Hole.

They all look at Mildred in wonder.

Arthur   [*incidentally*] You've seen a lot of films haven't you.

Mildred nods vacantly and looks into the distance, seeing the film in her head.

Dotty   We go to the pictures almost every week. They're showing To Catch A Thief

tomorrow night at the Regent.

Joey   That's supposed to be a great film. Wouldn't mind seeing that myself. One of

Hitchcock's, isn't it?

Mildred   That's right. Cary Grant and Grace Kelly. [*Dreamy*] It's supposed to be *very*

romantic.

Arthur   [*to Dotty*] Maybe we could join you if you like? Make a foursome?

Mildred   Are you sure you won't get into trouble?

Joey   [*placatory*] Oh no. Sergeant McCleary thinks of us as one of the family. Isn't that right

Arthur?

Arthur   Definitely. I'm like the son he never had.

Joey   [*incidentally*] Or wanted.

Dotty   What do you think Mildred?

Mildred   Don't see why not. [*Looks to Joey*] Now that we've got to know each other. It *would* make a nice change.

Joey   Now you're talking.

Arthur   That's settled then. We'll make a night of it. A few drinks after? Perhaps a bite to eat?

Dotty   [*smiles knowingly at Arthur*] Sounds perfect.

Arthur   [*looks tenderly at Dotty*] Perfect.

Mildred   [*sadly*] And then you'll be off to Germany.

Joey   Let's not think about that.

Dotty   [*distant*] For two years...

Arthur   Joey's right. Let's pretend it's not happening.

Dotty   Enjoy the moment?

Arthur   [*poignantly*] Enjoy the moment... You wouldn't want to see Joey cry. It'll be like Bambi all over again.

Joey   Do you *have* to keep bringing that up?

Arthur   [*to Dotty and Mildred*] It's a date then?

Dotty   [*looks to Arthur with soulful eyes*] I suppose it is.

Arthur   [*returns soulful look to Dotty*] Great...

                 Pause.

Mildred   We'd best think about getting back.

| Joey | How far *is* your place from here? |

| Dotty | It's a few miles. |

| Joey | [*looks to the sky*] It's a nice evening. Why don't we walk it? [*Looks to Arthur*] We can be your escort. |

Dotty and Arthur nod their agreement.

| Mildred | [*indignant*] With *my* feet? |

| Joey | Well… yes. Unless you've got some wings hidden under there? You haven't have you? |

Mildred rubs her feet.

| Mildred | But my feet are all swollen. I won't be able to walk three yards let alone three miles. I'll be on my feet all day tomorrow. [*Pause*] You'll have to carry me. |

| Joey | *Carry* you? For three miles? |

| Arthur | [*to Joey*] A Piggyback. |

| Mildred | Unless of course it would be too much for a big strapping soldier like you? |

Joey considers and becomes prey to flattery.

| Joey | [*now bursting with machismo*] I've done twenty mile hikes with full *kit* before now. Isn't that right Arthur? |

| Arthur | [*more to himself*] Not with eight pints down your neck you haven't. |

Joey turns his back to Mildred, bends a little, and puts his hands to his side in readiness for his passenger.

| Joey | [*to Mildred*] Climb aboard. |

Mildred   Are you sure? [*Pause*] I did have fish and chips earlier.

Mildred begins her run just as Joey turns around.

Joey   Of course I'm-

Joey catches Mildred full on and a tender moment is shared between them.

Mildred   Oh…

Joey   Sure…

Mildred   [*naively*] Whoops…

Dotty   Come on you two. [*Links arms with Arthur*] Let's make a move.

Joey slowly lets Mildred down.

Joey   Let's try again.

Joey turns and Mildred successfully jumps on him for a piggyback.

Arthur   [*to Dotty*] Louis, I think this is the beginning of a beautiful friendship.

Dotty looks puzzled.

Joey   What? [*Pause*] Are you stark raving mad?

Arthur looks to Mildred.

Arthur   Mildred?

Mildred   It's a line from Casablanca by Humphrey Bogart to Claude Rains. So… inspiring.
So… romantic

They begin their long walk.

Joey   [*looks to Arthur, disgruntled*] So… full of shite.

Arthur, Dotty, Joey and Mildred exit stage left as lights fade on them.

We are returned to Arthur's flat, elevated stage left, Christmas 2018.

Arthur still sits at the table looking out in wistful nostalgia.

Arthur   It took two hours to get to their place, Merlin, *and* we got caught in the pouring rain. Slashed it down. [*Smiles fondly*] It was certainly a night to remember. It seemed to be a more… *innocent* time back then. A lost world, you might say. [*Pause*] But I suppose everybody thinks that, when they've grown old. We didn't have two pennies to rub together in those days, but we got by… just. [*Looks briefly at Merlin*] It's never easy is it… being young? [*Takes sip from his drink*] Time goes so quickly, but at the time… [*Ponders deeply*] Strange that. One minute you're looking in the mirror and there's a young man full of beans looking back at you… the next it's some weary old fart on his last legs you hardly recognise... company accepted. But inside… your *spirit* perhaps… it's pretty much the same as it ever was. That's life I suppose. You just get on with it as best you can. [*Long Pause*] She was my first real love… Dotty I mean. [*Pause*] And my last… It's funny how things turn out isn't it? [*Long poignant pause*] Well… as I said, we eventually got to their place and they managed to sneak us in. They would have gotten into hot water if the matron had found out, that's for sure. But thankfully she never did...

Lights fade on Arthur's flat. It is 1955. Centre stage we see Dotty and Mildred's dining room, sparsely furnished and dimly lit. From far left, against the side wall is a kitchen door; a small dining table with four seats left corner; a bedroom door; a small settee beside which is a Dansette record player on a small stand; a small pile of LPs are on the floor in front of record player; a bathroom door; an armchair far right against the side facing out, to the right of which is another bedroom door.

Dotty, wearing yellow pyjamas and white slippers, stands to the left of the room, drying her hair vigorously with a towel. Mildred, wearing a pink nightie and fluffy pink slippers, enters from right bedroom door; her hair is wrapped up with a towel.

Mildred   Now I know what a drowned rat feels like. It was good to get out of those wet clothes. I was all… clammy.

Dotty   Thought that rain would never stop. Next time we go out we'll take brollies. Can't be too careful. [*Knocks on the bathroom door*] Are you two alright in there?

Arthur   [*calls out*] Sort of. We'll be out in a minute.

Joey   [*distantly to Arthur*] I feel a right lemon. This isn't exactly army issue you know.

Arthur   [*distantly to Joey*] Oh stop whinging. You're never satisfied. You *said* you wanted to be next to something soft and feminine.

Mildred and Dotty look to each other with stifled amusement.

Joey   [*distantly to Arthur*] I said I wanted to be next to some*body* soft and feminine; not some*thing*. That's completely different and you know it.

Arthur   [*distantly to Joey*] Never satisfied…

Enter Arthur and Joey, coyly, from the bathroom. Arthur is wearing Dotty's floral dressing gown and Joey is wearing Mildred's pink dressing gown. Dotty and Mildred eye up their guests with unfettered delight.

Mildred   Well… aren't you the pretty ones then?

Embarrassed looks from Arthur and Joey.

Dotty   [*to Arthur*] I think you look better in that than *I* do.

Arthur   [*lost for words*] Oh… thanks.

Joey   I feel a right prick.

Mildred   Say what you feel… don't hold back.

Dotty	It's only while your uniforms are drying in the airing cupboard. Besides, it's bad luck to wear damp clothes. They'll be ready in a few hours. Then you can make your way back to barracks before daybreak.

Dotty wraps her hair up with the towel.

Arthur	Well, I for one am grateful. You shouldn't have gone to all this trouble.
Dotty	It's the least we can do for our men in uniform. Can't have you looking all damp and scruffy. Besides… you look very sexy.
Arthur	[*vacantly*] Flatterer.
Joey	*I* don't feel very sexy.
Arthur	That's because you don't have the figure for it. Me… I feel *liberated.*

Dotty and Mildred laugh.

Dotty	Can I offer you a drink?
Joey	A beer wouldn't go amiss.
Mildred	We've only got tea or coffee.
Dotty	Or hot chocolate.
Mildred	We're not allowed alcohol, I'm afraid. The Matron inspects this place every so often.
Joey	Bit of a killjoy this Matron, isn't she?
Dotty	She rules with an iron fist.
Joey	[*to Arthur*] She belongs in the army more than *we* do. Maybe we should introduce her to Sergeant McCleary. A match made in heaven, I'd say.
Dotty	He wouldn't know what hit him. She's as tough as old boots.

Mildred   But she's a good sort. Deep down. She's like a mother hen, really.

Arthur   [*to Dotty*] A hot chocolate would be nice. Thanks.

Dotty   Pleasure.

Dotty and Arthur exchange knowing looks. Dotty exits, stage left, to kitchen.

Joey   [*to Mildred*] You seem to have a thing for pink.

Mildred   Oh, I'm sorry, is it not your colour? Perhaps you'd prefer purple with black polka dots?

Joey   [*emasculated*] Well... yes. [*Looks down at his apparel*] Obviously.

Mildred   [*to Arthur*] Never satisfied some people.

Arthur   Don't mind Joey. He's never happy unless he's miserable. He'll outlive all of us. It's always the grumpy ones that live a long life. Isn't that what they say?

Mildred   [*shakes head*] There's no justice in this world. [*Begins to exit towards her bedroom, stage right*] I need to finish drying my hair and then get some sleep. Make yourselves at home. [*To Joey*] Try not to slit your wrists while I'm gone.

Exit Mildred. Long pause as Joey looks smugly to Arthur.

Joey   Did you *see* the look she gave me? [*Disbelieving look from Arthur*] She fancies the pants off me that one. She was undressing me with her eyes. I felt... violated. [*Pause*] And it felt effing brilliant.

Arthur   [*looks Joey up and down disapprovingly*] You're such a cheap slut.

Joey   [*nodding*] Given half the chance.

Arthur looks around the room.

Arthur   Well... you heard Mildred. We may as well make ourselves at home.

Joey   This is the life. I could get used to this.

Arthur, from his vantage point, sees Joey's manhood.

Arthur   Oh, put it away Joey, for Christ's sake. It's like looking at a baby elephant.

Joey sheepishly closes his legs and pulls the dressing gown down over his knees in false modesty.

Joey   [*demure*] I was ventilating.

Arthur   You could get arrested for that you know… *ventilating*. They'd lock you up and throw away the key.

Joey   [*exasperated*] Just seeing me in this pink girlie *dressing* gown would be enough to get me banged up. [*Pause*] Exposing myself would just be the icing on the cake.

Long pause. Arthur is in deep thought.

Arthur   You're going to think me a fool…

Joey   [*nonchalantly*] What… in *that* outfit?

Arthur   I'm serious.

Joey   Okay. Why would I think you were a fool?

Arthur looks to Joey earnestly.

Arthur   Because I think I'm in love. [*Pause*] In fact I *know* I'm in love.

Joey   [*dismissively*] Fool.

Arthur   [*angrily*] I'll swing for you.

| **Joey** | Think about it Arthur. [*Pause*] We're off to Germany in a couple of days. Two years. Two sodding *years* we'll be away. You'll meet other girls. Besides… it wouldn't be fair on Dotty. |

Arthur contemplates long and hard.

| **Arthur** | [*resigned*] I suppose you're right. |

Dotty returns to the room with two steaming mugs of hot chocolate. Arthur and Joey rise to their feet.

| **Dotty** | You suppose who's right? |

Dotty hands Arthur his drink.

| **Arthur** | Oh… err... |

| **Joey** | We were talking about football. It's Manchester United versus Liverpool tomorrow night. I was saying to Arthur how Liverpool will win. |

| **Arthur** | [*unconvincingly*] Yes… that was it… Liverpool all the way… |

Dotty hands drink to Joey.

| **Dotty** | [*shakes head*] I will never understand the male species. [*Pause*] How grown men can get so excited about somebody kicking a ball around a field is beyond me. |

| **Joey** | [*lightly*] Men eh? |

Dotty looks around the room.

| **Dotty** | Right… I'd best turn in. We'll see you tomorrow night at seven. Don't be late. Let yourselves out. |

| **Arthur** | Great. We'll be off before sun-up. Thanks for the hot chocolate. And everything. |

| **Joey** | Night. |

Dotty   Night.

Arthur and Dotty exchange affectionate looks.

Arthur   [*gently*] Night.

Exit Dotty, stage left. Joey and Arthur speak in hushed tones.

Joey   That was a close call.

Arthur   Thanks Joey. You saved my bacon.

Joey   A good soldier never leaves his comrades behind.

Arthur   Now who's being John Wayne? But *Liverpool*? What's wrong with Arsenal? [*Pause*]
                And the football season hasn't even *started* yet.

Arthur and Joey resume their seats.

Joey   It was the only thing I could think of. Besides, you were drowning.

Arthur raises his mug in appreciation.

Arthur   I owe you one.

They drink some of their hot chocolate. Long awkward pause.

Joey   If I tell *you* something… promise me you'll never breathe a word?

Arthur   [*jokingly*] You're not going to tell me you're queer?

Joey   [*gently*] No.

Arthur   You wouldn't be the first. [*Pause*] Of course I won't breathe a word… to *any*body.
                We're mates, aren't we? Now… what did you want to tell me?

Joey looks worried.

| Joey | It's a little delicate. |

| Arthur | You've got the clap. |

| Joey | [*emphatically*] No. [*Sheepishly*] Far from it. |

| Arthur | Well… spit it out. |

| Joey | [*pensively*] Well… |

Pause.

| Arthur | Well? |

Long pause.

| Joey | [*awkwardly*] I've never… you know… *been*… with a girl before. [*Pause*] Never even had a girlfriend. |

| Arthur | [*blankly*] Oh… |

| Joey | [*bitter*] I *knew* I shouldn't have told you. |

| Arthur | [*placatingly*] No… I'm glad you did. |

| Joey | Really? |

| Arthur | Really. |

| Joey | You're not just saying that? |

| Arthur | Of course not. |

| Joey | Feels like a weight's been lifted off my shoulders. I felt sort of… *embarrassed.* |

| Arthur | There's nothing to be embarrassed about. [*Pause*] Besides… you're in good company. |

Joey looks to Arthur in surprise.

Joey   What… you too?

Arthur   [*resigned*] Me too.

Joey   [*exasperated*] Bugger me.

Arthur   No thanks.

Arthur and Joey laugh in blissful relief.

Joey   What a pair we are. [*Pause*] So what's *your* story?

Arthur shrugs his shoulders.

Arthur   I've never really met anyone that I wanted to be… *intimate* with. [*Looks to Dotty's bedroom door briefly*] At least not until now.

Joey   Well this is a fine affair. Here we are with two gorgeous girls in their beds not five feet away and we're dressed like some cheap tarts from soho drinking hot chocolate like a couple of old spinsters.

Arthur   Life is funny sometimes, isn't it?

Joey   Funny? [*Poignant pause*] It's effing tragic...

Arthur   And I'm not a cheap tart. I'm… *classy*, thank you very much.

Joey   If you say so.

Arthur   [*gently*] Get some sleep. [*Arthur switches off the light. Pale moonlight casts its magical glow within the room. As Arthur and Joey settle down to sleep, the door to Mildred's bedroom opens slightly; a faint light can be seen from the bedroom encroaching upon the room. Joey looks to Arthur in shocked awe. Long Pause*] Well?...

Joey anxiously rises from the armchair, elaborately smoothes down his dressing gown, breathes into his hand to check his breath, and then walks slowly and deliberately into Mildred's bedroom, closing the door softly behind him. Arthur smiles knowingly at Joey's rite of passage, and then looks to Dotty's bedroom door with a heavy heart; he holds a cushion close to him for comfort, as if he was embracing the woman he loved. Long pause.

Lights fade. We are returned to Arthur's flat, elevated stage left, Christmas 2018.

Arthur still sits at the table, now holding an empty glass in both hands, and looks out in sombre reflection.

Arthur   [*sadly*] I must have sat there looking at that door for the rest of the night. [*Smiles ruefully*] I was a young man who felt something new and exciting inside. My old mum was right. Your heart *does* skip a beat. [*Pause*] It does something to the brain, doesn't it, Merlin? Love. [*Pause*] Makes you weak like a kitten. I felt… overwhelmed. I couldn't sleep. I was a mess inside. She was all I could think of. And the clock was ticking. There was such little time left before we had to leave for Germany. I wasn't sure if she felt the same way or if I just imagined it but I knew my feelings for *her* were very real. [*He pours some whisky into his glass*] Needless to say, we were late back to the barracks and got a terrible rollocking from the sergeant, who put us on an instant charge. We were consigned to spud bashing as a punishment. It was one of the army's favourites for conscripts; that and scrubbing the floor with a toothbrush. When I think back now it was all very petty. Humiliating. Like sitting on a naughty step when you were a kid who was having a tantrum. But it's what we had to go through. [*Pause*] And we did…

Lights fade. It is 1955. Downstage centre we see the outside of an army kitchen. There are three small wooden benches, positioned in a semicircle facing out, in front of which are several opened cloth sacks of unpeeled potatoes and three large tin buckets.

Joey sits on the right bench; Eddie, a cockney who is sporting a black eye, sits on the middle bench, and Arthur sits on the left. Each has a small sharp knife and they are busy peeling potatoes and then throwing them into the tin buckets.

Eddie   I ain't never *seen* so many spuds. We'll be here a month of Sundays at this rate for sure.

Eddie briefly juts his chin out and rolls his shoulders as if punch drunk (he does this out of habit, sporadically).

Arthur   The sooner we get these peeled the sooner we can get gone.

Joey   [*angrily*] Sod this for a laugh.

Joey throws a peeled potato into a bucket dismissively.

Arthur   If we don't get them done quickly, we won't be out tonight.

Joey   [*defeatedly*] It's like chipping away at a *mountain*. I'll be an old man by the time we've finished. My balls will be scraping the *floor*.

Arthur   It could be our last chance to see the girls before we leave. [*Looks to Joey in desperation*] You *know* how much it means…

Joey   [*gently*] Yeah… course. [*Pause*] Me too.

Each peels with renewed vigour.

Eddie   In years to come they'll find three stiff old corpses in uniform still sitting here with a sack of mouldy old spuds unpeeled... and that'll be *us*.

Arthur   As long as we died trying.

Joey   So what did *you* do to honour us with your presence, Eddie?

Eddie   I was caught… [*slowly*] in fagrante… I *think* they called it.

Joey   In fagrante? What does that mean in English?

Arthur   In flagrante. It means he was having it off with somebody he shouldn't have.

Joey   [*to Arthur*] I didn't know you was bilingual Arthur? That poncy school education

                  of yours certainly paid off.

Arthur   [*to Eddie*] Please tell me it wasn't the company mascot?

Eddie   I've done some bad things in my life but a goat shagger I am not.

Joey   Anyone we know?

Eddie   I doubt it. Didn't even know her myself.

Joey   How is that possible?

Eddie   It was late. I was smashed. And so was she. I ended up in a club in Soho in the early

                  hours of the morning. Wardour Street I think it was. Got chatting to a young lady

                  at the bar. Very attractive... Mind you, after seven pints of special brew she could

                  have looked like Quasimodo for all I knew and I would *still* have thought she was

                  bangable. Quite posh I seemed to recall. She suggested we go back to her place.

                  [*Smiles to himself*] When we got there, we shagged like there was no tomorrow.

                  [*Pause*] I thought I was in love...

                  Wry smile from Arthur.

Arthur   [*nonchalantly*] And she was a prostitute.

Eddie   [*innocently*] I swear I did not have a clue that she was on the game.

Joey   You thought it was your suave charm and sophistication that attracted her to you?

Eddie   Well... yeah, *obviously*. That and the uniform.

Arthur   So how did you end up on a charge?

Eddie   Said she wanted payment for services rendered. Kicked up an almighty fuss when I told her I didn't have any money left. [*Looks to others*] You know what it's like. Nobody's got any money these days.

Joey   So what happened?

Eddie   Her pimp showed up, shouting and cursing, and we got in a hell of a scrap and somebody called the military police. They carted me off and … here I am.

Joey   And it was the pimp that blacked your eye?

Eddie shakes his head.

Eddie   One of the MPs clocked me with his stick. I was so smashed I didn't even feel it til I woke up this morning. [*Massages his eye*] Hurts like buggery now though.

Arthur   I think you've learnt a valuable lesson, don't you?

Eddie   Yeah. [*Thinks long and hard*] If you're going to get laid… make sure you don't get screwed.

Pause. Joey looks hard at Eddie.

Joey   Einstein's got nothing on you, has he?

Arthur   The real lesson is that you can't make a silk purse out of a sow's ear.

Joey and Eddie look puzzled.

Joey   What does that even *mean*?

Eddie   All I know is, yesterday I was just a boy from the Old Kent Road, and today… I'm a man who stands proud and tall from the university of life. [*Looks contrite*] Mind you… a man with itchy balls, a black eye and a hangover from hell.

Joey looks down at Eddie's crotch.

Joey   I'd get that looked at if I were you.

Arthur looks to Eddie with pity in his eyes.

Arthur   Was it really worth it though Eddie? Selling your dignity for a cheap night of forbidden passion? When all is said and done?

Eddie looks to Arthur as though repentant; he scratches his crotch.

Eddie   [*with sudden gusto*] Of *course* it was bloody worth it. [*Looks to Joey*] Is he always like this?

Joey   He likes to do things by the book does Arthur. Play by the rules.

Arthur   Without rules it would be anarchy.

Eddie looks to Joey and Arthur.

Eddie   So what's *your* story? What *you* been up to? Come on… spill the beans. I've given you *my* tale of woe. [*Pause*] Surprise me… I bet there's a vagina afoot?

Arthur   That *would* be a novelty.

Eddie   [*sagely*] When a man's in dire straits there's always a vagina. [*Earnestly*] If it wasn't for Juliet, Romeo would still be alive today.

Arthur looks at Joey in astonishment. Pause.

Arthur   He'd be wearing well.

Eddie   Mark my words. [*Accentuates with his knife*] It's like night follows day.

Joey   It's almost as if you've got psychic abilities, Eddie.

Eddie   I tell it as I see it. No point in fannying around. You can smell shite a mile away.

Arthur   [*incidentally*] You certainly can.

Pause.

Eddie   [to Joey] Well?

Joey   [*gingerly*] We met a couple of girls. Ended up spending the night and got back late. Simple as that.

Eddie   [*lustily*] Sweet. [*Pause*] Did you bang 'em?

Arthur   [*seriously*] A gentleman never tells.

Joey   [*triumphantly*] Well… seeing as I'm no gentleman… safe to say that *I* got my end away.

Eddie   Jammy bastard.

Arthur   [*gently to Joey*] Nobody likes a bighead.

Eddie   [*nudges Joey knowingly*] Any port in a storm, eh Joey?

Joey   Well… [*Glances nervously at Arthur*] You know how it is, Eddie.

Eddie   [*exuberantly vacant*] Yeah. [*Long expectant pause*] So how was it?

Arthur looks to Joey with disdain. Pause.

Joey   [*pensively*] It was like nothing I'd ever experienced before.

Pause.

Eddie   [*smirking*] First time, eh?

Joey sits up straight.

Joey   [*defensively*] No. Course not.

Arthur looks briefly to the heavens.

Arthur   [*to himself*] Saints preserve us.

Eddie looks consolingly to Joey.

Eddie   He's only narked 'cause he didn't get *his* leg over. [*Looks to Arthur*] Terrible thing…

jealousy.

Arthur   [*hurt*] It's just not something I want to talk about, that's all.

Eddie   She must have been a right ogre.

Joey   [*concerned*] Leave it Eddie.

Eddie   Is that what it was? A regular cyclops?

Eddie looks briefly to Joey but receives no response.

Arthur   Change the record.

Eddie   Did she have a bolt through her neck? [*Holds his arms ahead of him and adopts a

mad facial expression*] Like Frankenstein's monster?

Joey   Eddie-

Arthur   [*calmly to Eddie*] Word of advice.

Eddie   [*innocently*] Yeah? What's that?

Arthur looks lovingly at the knife in his hand.

Arthur   [*chillingly composed*] It is said that the best and most beautiful things in this world

cannot be seen or even heard, but must be felt with the heart. [*Long pause*] Unless

you want this knife up your arse where your brain is located, I'd keep a civil tongue

in my head if I was you.

Eddie is momentarily silenced in self-preservation. Long pause. He looks briefly to Joey as if for moral support and then exaggeratedly juts his chin out and rolls his shoulders. He continues to peel potatoes at a faster speed.

Eddie   [*blankly*] Some people are so touchy…

Lights fade. We are returned to Arthur's flat, elevated stage left, Christmas 2018.

Arthur smiles in weary reflection; the whisky is slowly beginning to take its toll.

Arthur   Poor Eddie. [*Pause*] As if his itchy crotch wasn't enough for him to contend with. I often wonder what happened to him. [*Looks to Merlin*] Do you think he became an old duffer like me? [*Pause*] Hard to imagine really. We were all so young back then. Has it really been sixty years? [*Long pause*] Time… where does it go, Merlin? [*Incidentally*] And in the blink of an eye. [*Pause*] We're all just *visitors* really, aren't we? Just passing through. [*Solemnly*] To the inevitable… [*Looks briefly above him*] It's good that I still have my memories. I'd be lost without them. So… *alone…* [*raises his glass to Merlin in melancholy*] company accepted. [*Sips from his drink*] Where was I? Ah yes… We managed to get through our little misfortune and made our rendezvous with Dotty and Mildred that evening with just minutes to spare. We were finally told that we were shipping out to Germany the next day so it was to be our last taste of freedom before the politicians took it away from us. [*Wistful*] For two years... All because our empire was weakened from the impact of so many conflicts. It was like a wounded animal. Damaged beyond repair. It couldn't cope without more boots on the ground. Suddenly we had to be the world's peacekeepers. But enough of that... It *was* to be our last evening together. [*Picks up glass of whisky*] You might call it the last supper…

Arthur drinks from his glass.

Lights fade. It is 1955. Dotty and Mildred's flat centre stage. Seated, in order, around rear and sides of the dining table, from right to left, are Arthur, Mildred, Dotty and Joey, finishing off their fish and chips. Dark bottles of beer are beside each plate; four emptied bottles of beer stand on centre of table.

Joey is the first to finish his meal and sits back with some satisfaction, patting his swollen stomach. The others continue to eat.

Joey   Cod and chips. [*Leans back extravagantly and looks up*] Food fit for the gods.

Joey takes a large swig from beer bottle. Mildred looks to Joey's empty plate.

Mildred   You certainly polished that off, Joey. Don't they feed you in the army?

Arthur   We must be the only regiment with a cook who *can't* cook.

Joey   It's true. His mash is like soup; bangers that could be used as truncheons; and his peas… like bullets. [*Looks to Arthur*] You could load your assault rifle with those things.

Arthur   And as for his spotted dick…

Dotty and Mildred share a knowing look.

Mildred   We could give him a cream for that.

The others laugh.

Dotty   I think that what you need is a woman to-

Arthur   [*dreamily*] How right you are.

Dotty   [*smiles at Arthur*] I was going to say… you need a woman to cook the meals for the men. Somebody like Fanny Cradock.

Mildred   She knows her onions that one. Very bossy to her poor husband Johnny, though. He looks hen-pecked. [*Looks concerned*] Has a very sad face.

Dotty   Poor Johnny. Mind you, he makes up for it with a glass or two…

Mildred   Or three.

Joey   Can't say I blame him. Perhaps it numbs the pain?

Arthur finishes his meal.

Arthur   [*shakes head*] A monocle… Who wears a monocle this day and age?

Arthur takes swig from his beer bottle.

Mildred   I think it makes him look distinguished. Like Cary Grant when he wears a cravat in To Catch A Thief. There's something very… English… about a cravat. Shows a certain… refinement.

Joey   He probably wears it to cover up the love bites from Grace Kelly.

Wry smiles from the others. Dotty finishes her meal.

Dotty   I think he's very dishy. [*Looks to Arthur*] I think you'd look nice in a cravat, Arthur.

Mildred finishes her meal.

Arthur   [*lightly*] I'll bear that in mind next time I'm in the French Riviera.

Dotty   When you're out of the army, I mean.

Awkward pause.

Arthur   [*sad*] Maybe I will at that.

Arthur looks endearingly at Dotty, who returns the favour.

Mildred   [*raises bottle of beer*] How about a toast?

The others raise their bottles. Long pause.

Joey   Well?

Mildred   [*unsure*] Seemed like a good idea at the time…

Dotty   To us.

Others   To us.

They each clink their bottles together and drink beer heartily.

Mildred   [*slightly tipsy*] And all who sail in her.

Quizzical looks from others.

Arthur   [*to Mildred*] I think somebody's been sailing too close to the wind.

Mildred takes a long swig from her bottle.

Dotty   Don't mind Mildred. Always happens with alcohol. She only has to smell the stuff
and she falls over.

Mildred   [*now overtly drunk*] That's very insulting.

Joey rises from his seat and beckons to Mildred.

Joey   Come on. [*Starts collecting the plates*] Let's go and wash up and then make coffee.
Think you might need one.

Arthur begins to rise.

Arthur   I'll give you a hand.

Joey gestures to Arthur with his hand, to stay. Arthur retains his seat.

Joey   We've got this covered, haven't we Mildred?

Mildred looks to Joey through narrowed eyes.

Mildred   Have we?

Joey   [*to Arthur*] Besides… I'm sure you two have a lot to talk about. [*Winks slyly at

Arthur which is seen by Dotty*] Come on Mildred. [*Now carrying all the plates and

cutlery, Joey exits into kitchen. Mildred stands in some confusion. Joey pops his head

out of the kitchen and looks directly to Mildred*] Pssst.

Mildred responds to Joey, and walks drunkenly to kitchen door. She turns to Dotty and

Arthur and waves childishly.

Mildred   Don't do anything I wouldn't do.

Exit Mildred.

Dotty   Seems to be a conspiracy.

Arthur   I think Mildred's too pissed to be part of a conspiracy.

Dotty   Maybe you're right. [*Pause*] What did Joey mean when he winked at you?

Arthur   [*slighly flustered*] Oh… you know Joey. Who knows what goes on inside that head of

his? [*Reflective pause*] He's a good egg though. A good friend. [*Rises, bottle in hand,

and walks towards record player*] Probably the best friend I've ever had. [*Picks up a

record from the pile of LPs and nonchalantly views the record sleeve*] I suppose that's

the one good thing about the army… you can make some good mates… mates for

life… hopefully.

Dotty   What is it you *want* out of life Arthur?

Arthur   [*shrugs*] Honestly? [*Long pause*] I don't want a life of regrets. [*Sombrely*] I don't

want to be an old man living out his days wishing that things had turned out better

than they did. [*We briefly see Arthur in 2013, in eerie light, who solemnly turns to his

younger self; light fades*] I suppose I want what my parents never had… a stable family life. A roof over my head. A place I can call my own. Nothing fancy. With somebody to share it with… [*looks sheepishly at Dotty*] for the rest of my life.

Long pause.

Dotty   [*emotional*] Sounds like heaven.

Long pause.

Arthur   [*looks to Dotty*] What do *you* want out of life, Dotty?

Dotty   Me? [*Looks to the heavens for inspiration*] I suppose the usual things. Kids. A husband who will love me for who I am and not what he expects me to be. [*Pause*] *My* parents should have given up years ago, but they stuck it out all the same. It must be difficult when times are hard. They're like chalk and cheese. I suppose it works for some people. They say opposites attract but I'm not sure it's true in their case. When Dad came back from the war he was a changed man. Hardened. Bitter. He lost his easy charm and his sense of humour. He must have seen some terrible things, but he never talked about them. Bottled it all up. Even now... after all those years.

Long pause.

Arthur   Never easy, is it? [*Pause*] Life... love.

Dotty   [*vacantly*] No…

Long pause.

Arthur   [*lightly*] Listen to us. We sound like a couple of old... fuddy duddies.

Dotty   We have our whole lives ahead of us.

Arthur   [*raises his bottle as in a toast*] We're young. [*Exuberantly*] The world is our oyster.

Dotty   I'll drink to that.

Dotty takes a long swig from her bottle.

Arthur   Careful. You don't want to end up like Mildred.

Dotty   I'm made of sterner stuff. [*Philosophically*] I am my Father's daughter.

Dotty has a look of concern on her face.

Arthur   Likes a drink, does he?

Awkward silence.

Dotty   [*sadly*] Yeah.

Dotty puts the bottle down on the table as though in guilt. Arthur senses her anguish and tries to lighten her load.

Arthur   Come and help me find some music. Must be something in here that fits the bill.

Dotty rises from the table and walks to Arthur.

Dotty   Okay. What sort of music do you like?

Arthur   Anything and everything. Something that sets the mood. You've got quite a decent collection.

Dotty picks up some records and leafs through them.

Dotty   It's mostly Mildred's. She's mad on American stars. Like Frank Sinatra and Johnnie Ray. Spends half her wages on records.

Arthur   Have you known each other long?

Dotty   Since school. She's the sister I never had, really.

Arthur   I like her. She's funny. One of a kind. [*Pause*] No brothers?

Dotty   Just me.

Arthur   Something else we have in common.

They gaze into each other's eyes and then kiss passionately. After a long moment Dotty breaks free and backs off a little.

Dotty   We shouldn't. I promised myself. You'll be off for two years. I can't get too attached. I mustn't. Don't you see? [*Tearful*] It wouldn't be right. It would make me an emotional wreck. [*Pause*] it would break my heart.

Dotty turns slightly away from Arthur.

Arthur   [*matter of factly*] I love you.

Dotty faces Arthur.

Dotty   [*gently*] I know.

Arthur looks lost in deep thought until he comes to a heartfelt decision.

Arthur   Marry me.

Dotty   [*bewildered*] What?

Long pause.

Arthur   [*subdued*] Marry me.

Arthur and Dotty face each other for what seems an eternity.

Lights fade. We are returned to Arthur's flat, elevated stage left, Christmas 2018.

Arthur looks on in pained reminiscence; an opened cigar box full of old letters from his distant past now sits in front of him on the table, beside which is his ubiquitous glass of whisky.

Arthur   It was the longest two years of my life, Merlin. [*Long pause*] She agreed to get engaged when I came back, *if* we both still felt the same. We wrote to each other every week. I've still got our letters. [*Picks up a letter from Dotty within the cigar box*] Every one of them. [*Closes his eyes briefly and smells the letter as though recapturing the essence of Dotty*] I can still smell her perfume… even now. After all this time. [*Long pause*] Two years. Seemed like a lifetime. [*Long pause*] Me and Joey were attached to the British Army of the Rhine in Bergen-Hohne. The Germans had been brought to their knees by the war. They were a spent force. The new threat now was from the Russians, because they had nuclear warheads. It was the beginning of the cold war… [*Pause*] Life was one endless round of drills, inspections, rifle practice, and manoeuvres; there were also lectures in the art of warfare, and all the while we were being constantly barked at by the NCOs. The only thing that got me through it all was when I received letters from Dotty…

Lights fade. It is January 1956. For theatrical effect a scrim (or gauze) is utilised. A pale light is focused on Arthur, centre stage right, who is sat up on his bunk within his barracks, reading the latest letter from Dotty; he is wearing a white vest, dog tags, and shorts. A pale hazy blue light is focused upon Dotty, centre stage left, who sits up within her bed, writing to Arthur on a notepad; she is wearing a nightdress.

    As Arthur reads, it is Dotty's voice that we hear.

Dotty   Dearest Arthur, Happy new year to you! I hope you were able to celebrate? We had a little party within the hospital late in the evening. Even Matron had a small glass of sherry. Imagine that! Although it was a happy occasion, I still felt sad that you weren't here. I miss you more than you will know. Three months have passed since you've been gone. Time seems to be going very slowly. Mildred sends her love. She and Joey still write to each other on and off. They seem well suited, don't they? I have at long last talked about you to mum and dad. Mum seems to approve but I'm not sure about dad. I don't think he likes the idea of his little girl growing up! Yesterday we had a ward sister give us a lecture on hygiene and she used a life sized dummy. It was the funniest sight. I do enjoy nursing but the days are very long. I still have at least another year of training before I become a "proper" nurse. Talk soon. Sleep tight. Lots of love, Dotty.

Light fades to pale blue on Arthur as a pale light is focused on Dotty. Arthur now writes to Dotty who reads the new letter.

As Dotty reads, it is Arthur's voice that we hear.

Arthur   Darling Dotty, I cannot tell you how comforting it is to read your letters these last months. The daily drudgery of army life continues to grate. We are up at six and kept active until late in the evening. Inspections are the worst. Everything is expected to be spic and span. If the Corporal can't see his reflection in our boots, he picks them up and throws them out the window. Me and Joey have both had this done to us. I have heard grown men cry themselves to sleep at night. Big men too. I won't give them that satisfaction. I heard that one poor soul hung himself in the latrine the other day. We were out on patrol a few days ago and found ourselves in the forest with full kit. Seeing the bluebells in full bloom raised my spirits. It almost made it bearable. I miss you terribly. All my love, Arthur.

Light fades to pale blue on Dotty as a pale light is focused on Arthur. Dotty now writes to Arthur who reads the new letter.

As Arthur reads, it is Dotty's voice that we hear.

Dotty   Dearest Arthur, You will have to excuse my letter as I have a bit of a cold and am not quite myself. Mildred says it's a summer cold and that everyone gets one. Mildred has been like a mother hen, making me chicken soup with lots of ginger. It tastes horrible but I don't let on! She's been a good friend to me has Mildred. I was on ward duty under the supervision of the ward sister the other day and sadly the elderly man who I had looked after only earlier had died suddenly later that day. I felt very upset as he seemed such a nice old man. Life is sad sometimes, isn't it? It's all part of

the job I suppose, and the ward sister said I shouldn't take it to heart. Easier said than

done. I wish you were here with me now, though I wouldn't want you to catch my

cold! Lots of love, Dotty.

Light fades to pale blue on Arthur as a pale light is focused on Dotty. Arthur now writes to Dotty who

reads the new letter.

As Dotty reads, it is Arthur's voice that we hear.

Arthur   Darling Dotty, It is nice to see the leaves start to turn brown as it means time is

marching on (no pun intended!) Although we rarely leave the camp, me and Joey

decided to go for a bracing swim in the Rhine at a bathing station near Bad

Gotesberg. The water was freezing! Joey showed how good he was at underwater

swimming and I showed off my diving skills. Joey must have caught a chill as he has

been laid low with flu like symptoms these last few days. We attended a lecture on

the Soviet threat to world peace the other day. A huge map showing Moscow and all

the major western cities it can strike with its nuclear missiles. I don't know what to

believe as the Russians were our allies and helped defeat the Germans. Stupid isn't

it? You are always in my dreams. All my love, Arthur.

Light fades to pale blue on Dotty as a pale light is focused on Arthur. Dotty now writes to Arthur who

reads the new letter.

As Arthur reads, it is Dotty's voice that we hear.

Dotty   Dearest Arthur, The festive season is supposed to be a time of happiness and

celebration, but I feel so sad to hear that Joey is still in hospital. Mildred is

heartbroken and writes to him every day. I know how wretched polio can be as we

have patients in isolation for such a very long time. It's a truly horrible disease. He

has told her to forget about him because he has lost the use of his legs, and doesn't feel like he's a real man anymore. He hasn't replied to her letters for quite a while

now. Poor Joey! Perhaps you can talk to him? You two are so close. Please give him

my love. I hope despite everything that has happened you are able to keep your

spirits up. Lots of love, Dotty.

Light fades to pale blue on Arthur as a pale light is focused on Dotty. It is Spring 1957. Arthur now

writes to Dotty who reads the new letter.

As Dotty reads, it is Arthur's voice that we hear.

Arthur   Darling Dotty, Joey is to be discharged next week and will be returning home in his

wheelchair. He is a shadow of himself. His disability seems to have taken his spirit

and now all he wants is to be left alone. I've tried to be the best friend I can but he

is very stubborn. I even took away an old luger pistol he'd acquired from the locals,

as I was worried for his own safety. I feel so bad that I can't do more for him. Life

isn't fair. He never deserved this. Nobody does. Time seems to be standing still, and

the six months I have left in this awful place is already starting to feel like an

eternity. My one salvation is hoping that you will be there when I get back. Please

say you will? They say absence makes the heart grow fonder and they are right. I

love you more after each passing day. All my love, Arthur.

Light fades to pale blue on Dotty as a pale light is focused on Arthur. Dotty now writes to Arthur who

reads the new letter.

As Arthur reads, it is Dotty's voice that we hear.

Dotty   Dearest Arthur, Some good news. I have finally passed my exams and am now a fully

fledged nurse. As is Mildred. I have never felt so proud as I do now. Wearing the

new uniform makes me feel suddenly very grown up! It is like a dream come true.

People even offer me seats on the bus. Can you believe it? Matron retired just the

other day and said that she was very proud of all of us and hopes that we continue in our duties for as long as she did. I felt a little tear run down my cheek, it was so moving. She never married, you know? After all this time. Of course, had she done so she would have had to leave the service. It's seems such a silly rule this day and age, doesn't it? I'm looking forward to seeing you again more than you could know. Lots of love, Dotty.

Light fades to pale blue on Arthur as a pale light is focused on Dotty. Arthur now writes to Dotty who reads the new letter.

As Dotty reads, it is Arthur's voice that we hear.

Arthur   Darling Dotty, Three months. Three months and my time here will be done. Finally. It feels like an important part of my youth has been somehow taken from me. Stolen. Time that I should have spent with you. You have been my one salvation. You have kept me sane through all this insanity. I hope you still recognise me when we meet again and that I haven't changed too much. I'm a little older. A little more cynical than I was. I'm probably more of a grouch than I was before! I hope you can put up with me? I will treasure all the wonderful letters that I received from you til my dying day. My love for you remains as strong now as it was when we last met. If anything it is stronger. I want to be with you so much that I think my heart might break. My one hope is that you still feel the same? All my love, Arthur.

Light fades to pale blue on Dotty as a pale light is focused on Arthur. Dotty now writes to Arthur who reads the new letter.

As Arthur reads, it is Dotty's voice that we hear.

Dotty   Dearest Arthur, We are soon to be reunited. Now just a matter of weeks. Imagine! It has been a long while, hasn't it? So much water has passed under that lonely bridge and yet here we are. Our destination finally in sight. Despite the distance that has been between us, my feelings for you have remained true. They say that love is blind.

But my eyes have been wide open these last two years. I have missed you so much and find myself tearful when thinking about you. But when I read your letters, it has been as though you were somehow here with me. It has been a comfort to me in a world that is sometimes dark and unforgiving. When I think of our future together I am like a butterfly who has just discovered its wings and is floating in the breeze for the first time. You may think this silly. But I can't seem to help myself. Lots of love, Dotty.

Lights fade.

End of Act One.

ACT TWO

Soulful music

Christmas 2018. Arthur's flat, elevated stage left.

> *Arthur slowly closes the cigar box. A sad smile is etched upon his weary face. He looks briefly to Merlin.*

Arthur   National Service was completed and I was finally demobbed. They provided me with an ill-fitting suit, but I was grateful for it at the time. I had precious little money. I was finally going home. [*Long pause*] Me and Dotty became engaged. We used a ring that was left to my mother by my Gran. It seemed like our lives were just beginning. [*Pause*] Her father disapproved of me for some reason and we never really hit it off. But it was a mutual… *detachment*. I managed to get a job as a clerk in an insurance company. It was a low paid position. Not what I expected to do for a living but it was at least a steady job with a chance of long-term promotion. I was lucky. Plenty of others struggled to get employment. I worked my arse off, Merlin. Kept my head down and got on with it. It's what you did in those days. [*Long pause*] I managed to track my old mate Joey down. We paid him a visit. He was down on his luck. He was living in cheap lodgings. [*Smiles reflectively*] Poor bastard didn't know what hit him when we turned up on his doorstep…

Lights fade. It is July 1958. Centre stage a darkened sparse room in a cheap lodging-house.

> *Joey, wearing a stained white vest, dark trousers and brown shoes, is sat in his wheelchair, stage left, listening to music on the radio while occasionally swigging beer from a bottle; his chin is stubbled with unkempt bristly growth. The sound of the door being vigorously knocked is heard. Joey switches off the radio, puts the bottle down on the table, and approaches the door, stage right.*

| **Joey** | [*impatiently*] Alright. Al*right*. God almighty. [*Pause*] I'm coming. Are you trying to break the sodding door down? [*Opens door*] This had better be- |

Standing at the door are Arthur and Dotty. Arthur is wearing a light casual suit with open necked shirt, cravat and black shoes; Dotty is wearing a bright summer dress, necklace and high-heeled shoes.

| **Arthur** | [*solemnly*] Hello Joey. Long time no see. |

| **Dotty** | [*smiling*] Joey. |

Joey is temporarily lost for words.

| **Joey** | Bugger me. [*Pause*] It's *you*. |

Arthur lets himself in, followed by Dotty.

| **Arthur** | You always did have a way with words. [*Looks around the room*] I would say nice place you've got here, but I'd be lying. |

Joey closes the door and faces Arthur and Dotty.

| **Joey** | It's a dump. But it's cheap. [*Pause*] How did you find me? |

| **Arthur** | I made a few enquiries. Pulled a few strings. Wasn't hard. |

[*Long pause*]

| **Dotty** | [*gently*] How *are* you Joey? [*Lying*] You look well. |

| **Joey** | I'm a cripple. [*Downcast*] I will *always* be a cripple. [*Incidentally*] This is as good as it gets. [*Looks Dotty in the eye*] How would *you* feel? |

Dotty looks to Joey with guilt in her eyes.

| **Dotty** | [*resigned*] Probably the same. |

Arthur looks about the room.

Arthur   What do you do all day? [*Pause*] How do you keep yourself busy?

Joey   [*blankly*] I listen to the radio. I read. I drink. [*Pause*] I have a lot of time on my hands. [*Poignantly*] A *lot* of time. [*Long pause*] What are you doing here, Arthur? Why are you wasting your time on *me*? You must have better things to do. [*Dismissively*] Look… maybe it's best if you just leave?

Arthur looks angrily to Joey.

Arthur   Is that what you really want?

Joey   [*subdued*] Yes.

Pause.

Arthur   [*loudly*] Well screw *you*.

Dotty   [*distraught*] Arthur-

Arthur   [*dismissively*] No. If he wants to be a dickhead for the rest of his life, let him. Why should we waste our time on a loser like *him*?

Arthur begins to walk to the door.

Joey   [*angrily*] You're lucky I'm in this wheelchair, Arthur. I swear if I wasn't you'd be spark out on the floor.

Arthur stops in his tracks, turns, and faces Joey.

Arthur   You're angry?

Joey   Of *course* I'm angry. Who wouldn't be?

Arthur   Then *be* angry. But don't live your life like… *this*.

Joey   That's easy for you to say. You don't know what I've had to go through.

Arthur   Well?

Joey   [*emotionally*] You have no idea- [*Pause*] What it's like. Day in, day out. Always the same.

Arthur   [*quietly*] Then tell me.

Joey looks pleadingly up at Arthur and then briefly at Dotty.

Joey   [*bewildered*] I don't know if I can…

Dotty   Try, Joey. [*Pause*] Please?

Long pause.

Joey   I wake in the morning thinking I can just get out of bed and walk to the bathroom. And then it slowly dawns on me. The realisation that those days are gone. It's like a broken record. This happens to me every day. Can you imagine what that's like? [*Pause*] It's torture. It's the everyday things. Things I took for granted that are now… impossible. Like walking up and down stairs. Running to catch a bus. Playing football in the park. Going for a swim. [*Poignant pause. Shakes his head*] Everything has to be on ground level. I have to look myself in the mirror every day and try to come to terms with being unable to walk. I keep telling myself that this is my life now. To accept being stuck in this… chair… for the rest of my life. Before, I had everything to live for. [*Pause*] But now… [*Pause*] Sometimes I wish that I could go to sleep… and never wake up.

Pause.

Arthur   And this is what it's going to be? Feeling sorry for yourself. For the rest of your life? You're young, Joey. You've got to think to the future no matter how bleak it looks now. It can only get better.

Dotty   Arthur's right, Joey.

Joey   It's a life sentence. There's no going back to how it was.

Arthur   Sometimes you have to play the cards you're dealt with. Even when it's a bad hand. As best you can.

Joey looks despondently at Arthur.

Joey   It's a busted flush Arthur. [*Shakes his head in defeat*] You don't understand. How could you?

Dotty   You can get through this, Joey. I *know* you can. I've seen so *many* struck down with this horrible disease. [*Chokes on her words*] Children. Young children… Don't give into it. [*Pause*] you have to fight it. [*Pause*] You *have* to.

Arthur   Dotty's right. Don't let it beat you.

Long pause.

Joey   [*composed*] Why did you come? Why are you wasting your time on *me*? You have your *own* life to live.

Arthur looks Joey in the eye.

Arthur   A good soldier doesn't leave his comrades behind.

A spark of reminiscence pricks Joey's conscience. Long pause.

Joey   This isn't the Rio Grande, Arthur. [*Pause*] It's Peckham.

Arthur   It's been a while, hasn't it?

Joey looks long and hard at Arthur and Dotty.

Joey   If I'd have known you two were coming, I'd have had a shave.

Arthur solemnly approaches Joey and offers his hand.

Arthur   It's good to see you again, Joey.

Pause. Joey warmly shakes Arthur's hand. Dotty tries in vain to conceal her emotions.

Joey   [*impassively*] Likewise.

Long pause.

Arthur   We have some news. [*Glances at Dotty*] Don't we?

Dotty smiles broadly through her tearful eyes.

Dotty   Yes. We do.

Arthur approaches Dotty and puts his arm around her shoulder.

Arthur   We're getting married.

Joey stares at Arthur and Dotty.

Joey   Married? [*Pause*] I don't know what to say.

Dotty   How about congratulations?

Joey   Of course. [*Opens his arms out to Dotty who bends down and receives a kiss*] I'm happy for you both.

Joey shakes Arthur's hand.

Arthur   I want you to be my Best Man, Joey.

Joey   Me?

Dotty   We insist. [*Adamant*] We won't get married unless you're there.

Arthur   What do you say?

Long pause.

Joey   I'll be honoured to be your Best Man, Arthur.

Arthur   Then that's settled. [*With relief*] Mission accomplished.

Dotty looks at Arthur with concern etched on her face.

Dotty   Not quite, Arthur?

A spark of recognition from Arthur.

Arthur   Of *course*. I'd forget my head if it wasn't screwed on tight. [*Arthur goes to front door and slowly opens it*] There's somebody who's been waiting patiently outside to see you.

Mildred is standing in the doorway; she is dressed in a light pink summer dress, with matching high heels.

Mildred   [*gently*] Joey.

Joey looks at Mildred in stunned disbelief.

Joey   Mildred…

Mildred rushes to Joey and kneels by his side, tenderly embracing him.

Mildred   Oh… Joey.

Joey   [*emotional*] Mildred...

Mildred and Joey kiss passionately and rekindle their friendship. Arthur and Dotty smile knowingly at each other; they exit stage right and close the door gently behind them.

Lights fade. We are returned to Arthur's flat, elevated stage left, Christmas 2018.

Arthur   It was a beacon of light in an otherwise grey world, Merlin. We brought Joey back from the brink. With love. And understanding. Traits that were hard to come by back then. [*Solemnly*] Perhaps they always have been. [*Long pause*] Time. [*Looks briefly to Merlin*] Where does it go? It's like a black hole, isn't it? Days that never seemed to end come and gone as though they never really existed. Like a mad magician's sleight of hand. All now just memories. [*Pause*] It's hard to believe we were ever young. But I know we *were*. [*Long pause*] After we married we lived with Dotty's parents – it was only to be until we could afford our own place. She had to give up her career in nursing. That couldn't have been easy for her. It was a different time back then. But she never complained. It wasn't in her nature. But I know it hurt. She managed to get a job as a receptionist. I remained office bound. I was now firmly part of the rat race. I hated it but I did the best I could. We tried to save as much as possible from our meagre wages for a deposit on a house. It wasn't easy. [*Long pause*] There were times when it felt like an eternity...

Lights fade. It is late evening in August 1959. Dotty's parents' dining room centre stage. Dimly lit and cramped, it is a typical room for a mid-terraced family home of its time.

shoes; Dotty is wearing a floral belted dress with light shoes. An interminable silence is punctured by Arthur.

Arthur   A funny thing happened at work today. [*Gerald briefly unfolds the corner of his newspaper and gives Arthur a disapproving look. Arthur carries on regardless*] One of the men I work with, Philip, was walking past the telex machine with his cup of tea when he tripped. He ended up on the floor and the tea ended up in the machine. You should have seen the sparks that came out of that thing. It was like a firework going off.

Hilda   Oh dear, that does sound dangerous.

Gerald   [*to himself*] Bloody idiot.

Hilda   Gerald. Language.

A brief flick of the newspaper from Gerald in response.

Dotty   [*concerned*] Did he get into trouble, Arthur?

Arthur   Big time. The manager says they'll have to dock his wages. He was pretty close to being sacked on the spot.

Hilda   Seems a bit unfair. It was an accident after all.

Arthur   Those machines cost a fortune. Because we're a small company we've only got two of them. Now we've only got one. They're our lifeblood really. Most of the information we get comes from them.

Gerald   Life was a lot easier when people talked to each other rather than through *telexes*. Face to face. [*Dismissively*] And they call it *progress*.

Gerald continues to engross himself in his newspaper. Long pause.

| **Hilda** | Talking of progress… Mrs Henderson next door invited me over earlier this afternoon. Showed me their new television. Oh, it was marvellous. We watched The Adventures of Robin Hood. |

Gerald ruffles his newspaper in disgust.

| **Gerald** | [*scathingly*] Television… |

| **Dotty** | [*to Hilda*] Perhaps it's time *we* thought about getting a television, mum? They've got a sale on at Radio Rentals. Maybe we could get a good deal? On the never never. |

| **Hilda** | [*dreamily*] Well, there's a thought... Imagine that. Our own television… |

| **Arthur** | We'd chip in. Share the cost? |

| **Dotty** | [*to Gerald*] They're all the rage now, dad. |

| **Gerald** | We have a radio. What do we need a television for? [*Pause*] Two channels... They'll never replace radio. Besides, they cost an arm and a leg. We're not exactly made of money. Or hadn't you noticed? |

Arthur shakes his head in disbelief.

| **Hilda** | Maybe your dad's right? It's hard enough just keeping a roof over our heads. A television's a big commitment. |

| **Dotty** | But mum... |

| **Gerald** | We'll hear no more on the subject, young lady. When you're finally able to buy your own property you can buy a *dozen* televisions for all I care. Until then you'll have to make do with the radio. |

| **Dotty** | [*to herself*] Can't come soon enough. |

Gerald   Hmm?

Hilda   Dorothy. Don't be disrespectful to your father.

Gerald   [*to Hilda*] Putting fancy ideas in their heads. [*Ruffles his paper and continues to read*] Honestly, Hilda... [*Pause*] Television indeed.

Hilda looks downcast but carries on knitting. An awkward silence ensues.

Arthur   [*to Hilda*] Your knitting seems to be coming on a treat.

Hilda   Oh, thank you Arthur. It's just a cardigan. For Dorothy.

Dotty   Isn't mum clever, Arthur? [*Proudly*] She's the best mum in the world.

Hilda   [*elated*] Oh, stop it. [*Tearful*] You'll make me cry.

Gerald ruffles his newspaper. Arthur glowers at Gerald.

Arthur   Dotty's very lucky to have a mum as nice as you. We both are.

Long pause.

Hilda   [*now composed*] It's getting late, Gerald. [*Puts knitting down and rises from her seat*] We should be going up. Give these two lovebirds some peace and quiet.

Dotty rises and kisses her mother.

Dotty   Night mum.

Arthur   Goodnight.

Exit Hilda stage right. Gerald rises, folds his newspaper, and places it on the corner of the table and slowly faces his daughter.

Gerald   [*distantly*] There are times… when I forget what it's like to be young.

Long pause.

Dotty	[*softly*] Night dad.

Gerald nods, looks briefly at Arthur, and exits stage right. Long pause.

Arthur   What was *that* all about?

Arthur rises and walks to table to read the newspaper. Dotty resumes her seat.

Dotty   [*sentimentally*] The war...

Arthur glances at the headlines of the newspaper.

Arthur   That was *years* ago.

Dotty   It never leaves him.

Arthur   It gets on my nerves. It's hard enough we have to live with him. But that chip on his shoulder… it's bigger than Gibraltar.

Dotty   [*warily*] He'll hear you.

Arthur   I'm not sure I care anymore.

Dotty   It won't be forever.

Arthur   I'll be glad when we can finally move out. Live under our *own* roof. Seems to be taking a lifetime.

Dotty   I wonder if we'll end up like mum and dad?

Arthur   If I end up like *him* you have my permission to shoot me.

Dotty   I might hold you to that. [*Rises from her seat and accompanies Arthur*] What are you reading?

Arthur   Usual. Conflict. Death. The war in Vietnam. [*Looks to Dotty*] But the good news is that Julie Andrews has left Broadway's production of My Fair Lady to concentrate on her career on the big screen. It's got a bigger coverage than people being blown

up in that idiotic war. Beggars belief.

Dotty   *We* haven't been to the theatre in a long time.

Arthur   Or the pictures…

Dotty   [*wistfully*] Our first date.

Arthur   Seems so long ago now…

They face each other and kiss gently.

Dotty   One day we'll be an old married couple.

Arthur   Any regrets Mrs Peaty?

Dotty shakes her head.

Dotty   I can't think of anyone I'd rather be married to than you, Arthur.

Arthur   I loved you from the first moment I met you. I don't tell you nearly enough. [*Pause*]

I love you.

Pause.

Dotty   [*gently*] I know.

Arthur   This isn't forever you know. [*Looks briefly up at the ceiling and around the room*]

Us living here. We'll have our own place before long. You'll see.

Dotty breaks free from Arthur and looks around the room.

Dotty   Touch wood. It will be wonderful to have our own house. Our own little nest egg.

Our own roof over our heads. Imagine it. [*Pause*] Just the three of us...

Arthur continues to read the newspaper obliviously.

Arthur   The sooner we get our own place the better. [*Pause*] I see House Of Fraser have bought Harrods. Thirty seven million pounds. We could buy a big house for thirty seven million pounds, couldn't we?

Dotty looks to Arthur inquisitively.

Dotty   [*coyly*] I suppose we could.

Arthur   British Motor Corporation have produced a new car. It's called the Mini. Looks a neat little car. It's being sold all round the world. [*Pause*] Makes you proud to be British.

Dotty   [*blankly*] Yes, I suppose it does.

Arthur continues to read.

Arthur   Hawaii has been declared as the fiftieth state of America. It says here that it is the only US state situated outside of North America.

Dotty   [*quietly*] Really?

Arthur continues to read in silence. Long pause. He finally looks up from the newspaper and looks blankly ahead.

Arthur   [*nervously*] The three of us?

Dotty   [*feigning disinterest*] Hmm?

Arthur looks to Dotty who returns his gaze. Long pause.

Arthur   [*dumbstruck*] The *three* of us?

Dotty nods proudly. They both smile adoringly at each other. Long pause.

Lights fade. We are returned to Arthur's flat, elevated stage left, Christmas 2018.

Arthur holds a framed photograph of a new born baby in his hands and views it with sadness; he places it on the table facing him.

Arthur   Who would have thought? [*Pause*] I was going to be a father? I was as proud as punch that day, Merlin. [*Tops his glass with whisky*] It was the happiest day of my life. [*Arthur downs all the whisky from his glass; his speech is now slightly slurred*] You never know what's round the corner in life, do you? One minute you're as high as a kite. [*Long contemplative pause*] The next you can be on your knees in despair... Life is funny that way, isn't it? The way it gives in one hand and takes in another. Just when you think you've finally cracked it. When you think you're invincible... life has a way of reminding you... of just how fragile... we *all* really are...

Lights fade. It is May 1960. A single room in a hospital maternity ward centre stage. The sounds of other babies crying are heard in the background.

Dotty, clearly very weak, is lying in bed cradling her new-born baby boy who sleeps peacefully. The attendant nurse ushers Arthur in from stage right. Arthur sits beside Dotty and gently strokes her hair.

Nurse   I'll just be outside. [*To Arthur*] I'm afraid I'll have to limit your visiting time. [*Concerned*] Your wife has lost a lot of blood, mister Peaty, and is feeling very frail. She'll need plenty of rest.

Arthur   [*to nurse*] She's going to be alright, sister?

[*Long uncertain pause*]

Nurse   [*nods*] With lots of peace and quiet. [*Worried look to Dotty*] We'll keep a careful eye on her.

Exit nurse stage left.

Arthur   They kept me out there for *hours*. I felt like I was going mad with worry. All sorts of scenarios were playing in my head. I was thinking the worst. Oh Dotty… you look so weak. [*Feels her brow*] You're burning up.

Dotty   They had to give me a c-section. Then they couldn't stop the bleeding. [*Long pause*] Oh, Arthur, I'm so tired...

Arthur   My poor darling…

Dotty tries to lift up the baby but is too weak.

Dotty   Come and say hello to your son.

Arthur carefully picks up his son.

Arthur   My *son*? [*Arthur sees his son for the first time*] He's so beautiful. He has your eyes.

Dotty   [*smiles faintly*] He has your stubbornness. He didn't want to make an appearance.

Long pause.

Arthur   He's wearing your pendant.

Dotty   For luck.

Arthur smiles reflectively.

Arthur   You always were superstitious.

Dotty   He'll need all the help he can get. [*Pause*] It's a cruel world out there.

Arthur   Just having you as a mother is more than enough luck. [*Pause*] He's already blessed. [*Pause*] I'm so proud of you, Dotty. I love you so much.

Arthur is busy doting on his new baby.

Dotty   [*feebly*] I feel like I could sleep for a hundred years, Arthur.

Long pause.

Arthur   [*smiles*] Like sleeping beauty. [*Pause. Dotty is now seemingly asleep unbeknownst to Arthur*] I'll be the prince that wakes you with a kiss. I would gladly wait a hundred years for you, Dotty. I'd wait forever if need be. [*Sees that Dotty's eyes are closed*] That's it. Get some good sleep. You've been through so much. [*Arthur kisses Dotty's forehead. Concern is shown on his face*] You're cold. So cold. Maybe you need more blankets? That must be it. [*Lifts the blanket higher*] I'll get the nurse to bring more blankets. Perhaps a hot water bottle? [*Dotty is non-responsive*] Why are you so cold? Dotty? [*Turns to door*] Nurse. [*Pause*] NURSE. [*The nurse enters the room frantically and goes to Dotty's side*] My wife is cold. Like ice.

The nurse checks Dotty's temperature with her hand and then slowly pulls back the blanket, revealing massive bleeding. Dotty's gown and bed are saturated with blood. The nurse hurriedly ushers Arthur away and pulls the curtains round Dotty's bed, leaving a bereft Arthur outside, still holding the baby. The silhouette of the nurse frantically trying to resuscitate Dotty can be seen.

Nurse   [*shouts*] Doctor. DOCTOR. Please come quickly.

A doctor rushes into the room from stage right.

Doctor   What is it, nurse?

The sound of the new-born baby crying permeates the air.

Arthur   Dotty…

Nurse   [*desperately*] She's haemorrhaged, Doctor.

Doctor   Step back please nurse. We haven't much time.

Arthur   Please… No…

The doctor tries in vain to bring Dotty back to life.

Nurse   She's not responding.

Arthur   Somebody…

Long pause.

Doctor   She's beyond help. [*calmly*] There's nothing we can do.

Nurse   But surely, Doctor?...

Doctor   Her lungs have filled with blood.

Nurse   Dear god…

Long pause.

Doctor   I'm afraid she's gone…

Arthur looks to the heavens. The sound of babies crying gets louder.

Arthur   No. PLEASE? Anything but *this*. Take *me*. Not *her*. Why are you *doing* this? You bastard. She never harmed a fly. [*Echoed screams in desperation*] PLEASE... NO...

Lights fade. We are returned to Arthur's flat, elevated stage left, Christmas 2018.

An emotional Arthur sits at the table, drunkenly looking out in despair. In his hand is the luger pistol that he took from Joey back in 1957.

Arthur   She drowned in her own blood, Merlin. She was in the prime of her life. She didn't get to live out her life as I have. And I've lived with the guilt all these years. Every day. If she hadn't met me she would have been content as a nurse which is what she dreamed of since she was a girl. I ruined her life. I robbed her of her future. [*Pause*] Went off the rails. Couldn't cope. Took to the drink. Ran away from it all. Ran away from all my responsibilities. Wondered the streets of London. Was homeless. For *years*. I no longer cared about anything. Or any*one*. For a long time… Talking to you has brought it all back. All the hurt. The guilt… I kept Joey's gun all these years. Who would have thought? [*Lifts gun and examines it*] All those I knew when I was young… [*Shakes head despondently*] All gone. Dotty was right. Life *is* cruel. [*Pause*] It doesn't seem right… that I should have lived such a long life… when hers was cut so short…

Arthur slowly points the gun to his head and closes his eyes.

Lights fade.

EPILOGUE

Spring 2019. Centre stage. The small dark flat, once occupied by Arthur, has now been virtually cleared by Felix and Bill. A few full bags on the floor are all that remain from Arthur's existence.

Bill stands centre stage right tying a full bag of clearance debris, as Felix enters from centre stage left, dragging a full bag.

Bill   Just these last bags to clear and our work is done. Then they can fumigate the place. [*Pause*] You were right Felix.

Felix   [*subdued*] About what?

Bill looks around the room.

Bill   Now that this place has been cleared there is a sense of purpose after all.

Felix smiles vaguely.

Felix   Sounds like I'm leaving this job in safe hands.

Bill   At least the charity shops will do alright. That old record player of his must have been worth a few bob. Collectable records too.

Felix   At least somebody will benefit from his death.

Bill   It's amazing what you find, isn't it? [*Pause*] Who'd have thought that we'd have found that old pistol hidden away?

Long pause.

Felix   [*solemnly*] And still fully loaded.

Bill   Wonder where he got it?

Felix   [*shrugs*] We'll never know. We'll let the police figure that one out.

Bill   It was pretty old. More than likely blow your hand off firing that old thing. Looked like an antique. Wonder why he kept it?

Felix   Part of his history I suppose. Must have meant something to him. Personal.

Bill   And what of *your* history Felix?

Felix   Hmm? Me?

Bill   I know so little about you, really. Are you married?

Felix   [*dismissively*] No. [*Pause*] I've always preferred my own company. Bit of a loner, I suppose.

Bill   No brothers or sisters?

Felix shakes his head.

Felix   I'm the last in the line. I think I was more than enough for my foster parents.

Bill   You were adopted? Weren't you ever curious? [*Felix looks quizzically at Bill*] To find out who your real parents were?

Felix   My real parents didn't want me. I'm sure they had their reasons. [*Pause*] I chose not to know… To let sleeping dogs lie. I can't complain. [*Pause*] My adoptive parents treated me as one of their own. I had a good upbringing. No regrets.

Bill   And you've nothing to show for it? [*Puzzled look from Felix*] Your *real* parents, I mean?

Felix   Just an old Saint Christopher. It was my mother's. [*Pause*] I've worn it all my life. For luck.

Felix momentarily lifts the Saint Christopher from his neck and rubs it between his fingers. Awkward pause. Bill looks out the window.

Bill   You'd need a good head for heights living this far up. Think I'll keep my feet firmly on the ground rather than up in the clouds.

Felix   It's closer to your Maker I suppose. Perhaps a little *too* close.

Bill   So how does it feel?

Felix   Hmm?

Bill   This being your last day.

Long pause.

Felix   It feels odd. [*Long pause*] Not the way I thought I'd feel at all.

Bill   How did you *think* you'd feel?

Felix   I thought I'd leave satisfied that I'd done the best I could, but I feel as though a part of me has somehow been lost. I feel... empty. Strange. I've never felt like this before up until now. [*Long pause*] Can't put my finger on it.

Felix looks around the emptied room as if searching for answers.

Bill   You've done a good job over the years, Felix. A hell of a service to the community. You should feel *proud* of all you've achieved.

Felix   I *am* proud of all the work I've done in the past.

Bill   Then why would you feel empty?

Felix thinks long and hard.

Felix   Perhaps it's because of all the poor souls who have died... All alone... We call ourselves a community... Nobody deserves to be left on the shelf. To fend for themselves. Isolated. Desolate. Sad. [*Shakes head*] We should be in this together. [*Pause*] There are thousands of faceless people out there in every corner of the land starved of companionship... Young and old. Male and female. They all have their own unique story. And yet we often choose to ignore them. It's such a simple thing. To show compassion. To reach out. To those whose needs are greater than our own. But we remain blinkered. [*Pause*] Forever looking out for ourselves. [*Pause*] But when it's *our* turn to leave this life… who's to say *our* fate will be any different to theirs? [*Pause*] If nothing changes…

Felix and Bill look to each other in deep thought.

Lights fade.

Play ends.

Playwright: **Colin Fantham** BA (hons)

Colin Fantham was born in Stratford-upon-Avon in 1957. Having spent over 40 years in the insurance industry he is now retired and devotes most of his energy to his writing. Creative from an early age, Colin has written several pieces of music and numerous scripts for stage and screen.

Some other examples of his work:

Henry's Last Act ©. A half hour original comedy series for television. It is set in The Sunny Retreat retirement home for entertainers. This gentle comedy centres around the friendship between residents Henry, Edgar and Twinky, as well as an abundance of other quirky characters, including Jessica who is a teenage work-experience employee. Eight episodes. PublishNation – various distribution.

Visitors from a Lost World (film script) ©. Based on a short play by the same author. During a death clearance in a remote tower block flat, somewhere in London, the past of its former resident, Arthur, comes hauntingly to life. We see Arthur when he served his national service in the 1950s, when he met and fell in love with Dotty. This is their story. PublishNation – various distribution.

Colin Fantham is a member of WriteOn script workshop in Cambridge, a candidate member of Writers Guild of GB, and a member of Geoffrey Whitworth Theatre.

www.ingramcontent.com/pod-product-compliance
Lightning Source LLC
Chambersburg PA
CBHW080757030726
47598CB00007B/2614